THE MAGIC OF FINDHORN

THE MAGIC OF
FINDHORN

Paul Hawken

SOUVENIR PRESS

828/354

Illustrations by Margo Herr.

Grateful acknowledgment is made for permission to reprint excerpt from *The Waste Land* in *Collected Poems 1909–1962* by T. S. Eliot, copyright, 1936, by Harcourt Brace Jovanovich, Inc.; copyright, © 1963, 1964, by T. S. Eliot. Reprinted by permission of the publishers.

First published in the U.S.A. by Harper & Row

First British Edition published 1975
Reprinted March 1976 by
Souvenir Press Ltd, 43 Great Russell Street, London WC1B 3PA

ISBN 0 285 62175 0

Reproduced Photolitho in Great Britain by
J W Arrowsmith Ltd, Bristol

Contents

Dedicated to
Ann
whose spirit
was the real author

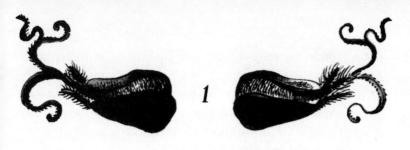

To the Kingdom of the Wind

There have been stories in the press and other media about a small community in the north of Scotland called Findhorn where people talk to plants with amazing results —stories of vegetable and flower gardens animated by angelic forms where Pan's pipes are heard in the winds— stories of plants performing incredible feats of growth and endurance: 40-pound cabbages, 8-foot delphiniums, and roses blooming in the snow—all a short distance from the Arctic Circle—Don Juan and Tolkien combined, where the elemental world of plants and animals cooperate with fairies, elves, and gnomes in creating a land where nothing is impossible and legends are reborn; people heard talking to plants and angels in a casual and informal way, creating a Garden of Eden where only gorse bushes and spiky grass grew before; a cold windblown peninsula jutting into the North Sea with soil as sandy and worthless as your local beach; a community said to be run and operated under messages and guidance received from God through Eileen Caddy, the wife of its founder, Peter Caddy.

With those sketchy and unbelievable tales, I left America for Scotland to search out the Findhorn Gardens. What I found seems larger than a 40-pound cabbage. Fairies and elves seem tame stuff compared to what one experiences

there. Findhorn may be a manifestation of a light and
power which could transform our planet within a lifetime,
or it could be an illusory bubble on the troubled waters
of the world civilization that will burst, leaving no traces.
A born skeptic, I can appreciate that much of what you
will read will seem implausible and incredible. I do not
ask that you believe this account, for it is written only
through one man's eyes. Every aspect of creation has as
many realities as perceivers. The fullness of an autumn
moon through a million pairs of eyes is then a million
different moons while remaining but a single moon. And
so it is with Findhorn. Peter Caddy has said: "You cannot
describe Findhorn; people must experience it themselves
in order to understand it."

"Second sitting, last call," cried the steward, hurrying
through the second-class coach on the crowded train to
Inverness. The northbound *Royal Highlander* returning
tanned Scots from late summer holidays had scheduled an
extra meal to which the elderly trio in my compartment
hungrily responded, leaving me alone to ponder the misty
hills and fields outside the rain-streaked windows.

The small plots of stubble, sprouts, and "neeps," contained within mossy walls of broken stone, marched irreg-
ularly up the slopes, the absence of trees and bushes giving
them an air of frugality and spareness, as if nothing was
wasted, nothing was frivolous, all was being used. A tired-
looking field hand encased in tattered tweeds and baggy
gabardine walked along the rocky borders of his oat-
field.

I had assumed the British to be a tired race exhausted
in a vain world conquest, a society wandering in the track-
less maze of cultural decline, and the cotter moving slowly
between the thin stand of oats with his head bowed to the
dirt seemed to carry his motherland's fatigue as his heritage. The continual cropping of oats and barley having

nursed the agricultural teats dry, the exhaustion of an empire was now mirrored in the glazed eyes of its tiller and in his croft of marginal soil which appeared as useless as a hag's breast in a nursery.

The facile thoughts of a "dead" empire which were nurtured and incubated in the dregs of a chauvinistic American postwar education had given way to elusive stories and shreds of evidence which spoke of a Britain strangely "alive." The books of John Michell and Alfred Watkins revealed a hierophantic script of "ley" lines inscribed across the face of the British Isles—a record hinting of forces and fields of energy that linked the stellar observatories of Stonehenge and Avebury to hundreds of cairns, cromlechs, dolmens, roads, fanes, and churches. I had read the older work of Evans-Wentz describing a Celtic culture as old as Carnac which had managed to survive into the twentieth century, a culture that could still contact and communicate with the fairies and little people. Fiona Macleod's books told about the prophecies of Iona and stories of the obscure Culdees who preserved Druidic knowledge and lore for centuries in secret colleges. But none of these prompted me to return to the land of my ancestors. Not until, on the very day I was packing up my desk to leave a job of seven years, a casual friend threw a crudely printed pamphlet on my desk and said I might be interested in it: "The Findhorn Garden—An Experiment in the Cooperation Between Three Kingdoms."

The name Findhorn had come up several times during the preceding year. Since I had been in the natural food and farming business for many years, sooner or later all mention in the media of alternative methods of agriculture crossed my desk. I remembered reading an article in *Harper's* by Peter Tompkins which mentioned the community of Findhorn, describing a small group of people, isolated on a cold windblown peninsula in Scotland, who were growing one of the world's most fantastic gardens with no resources except bushels of love and contact with another dimension of consciousness called the Devic and Elemental Worlds.

It was one of those stories that seemed to cut right through defenses and rationalizations, partly because it was so outrageous and partly because it seemed to embody in a living way many of the legends and myths of a very ancient island. Everything I had read of Britain spoke of the past, but in the story of Findhorn with its supernatural gardens and contact with the world of nature spirits, it was as if the ancient Druidic culture had sprouted again as suddenly as the staff of Joseph of Arimathea had become the Glastonbury thorn.

Reading it in the journalistically conservative *Harper's* caught me psychologically flatfooted and analytically agape. In my cluttered and shabby warehouse office in the old industrial section of Boston, I could not only see the rubbish skies of urban decay, but a large mythical body coming to life, snapping ropes of neat well-ordered thoughts and unloosening bonds of accepted "knowledge," silently mapping out with its gleaming eyes a fettered earth. It moved slowly from its long slumber, as if from the depths of space some stray cosmic force had broken its hibernation. It was the myth of creation and all the vital forces of life coming to the fore to challenge the one-sided clipboard theories of science, head on. Around it danced myriad creatures of a thousand myths—fairies, sylphs, dryads, elves, gnomes, and the god Pan, coming alive at Findhorn, where time was not speeding up but opening up and swallowing in a gulp "rules" and "laws."

After reading the *Harper's* article, I sent off photostats to friends, farmers, and agricultural experts. With few exceptions all seemed to ignore or dismiss it. It wasn't possible, they said. You needed soil, no matter what method was employed, and these people didn't even have soil. They were growing in sand.

I had worked with the earth for years and had seen some fantastic feats of horticulture, but none of them matched up to what was being intimated here—a garden growing in the sand and cold, producing sixty-five different vegetables, forty-two herbs, and twenty-one types of fruit. Even if they could be cultivated in that climate, the reports of 42-pound cabbages and 60-pound broccoli plants made it quite unbelievable. Peter Caddy, the founder of Findhorn, supposedly did not know much about gardening, having never planted a seed until he started his garden in the dunes, yet here he was growing things in unheard-of proportions and breaking all the rules as well. It would have been one thing for Peter Caddy to attribute his success to some ingenious technique of fertilization, but instead, I was presented with a picture of an ex-Royal Air Force squadron leader blandly and matter-of-factly ascribing his horticultural mastery to communication and cooperation with Devic presences, Nature Spirits, fairies, elves, and the legendary deity named Pan.

As the train moved north, the plants became more miniaturized, drawing back from the surface, hesitant and understated; shrunken trees, bracing themselves for the wintry blast soon to come, were twisted into unseemly contortions, their strange and submissive shapes bearing witness to their master like stumpy oak-leaved dwarves kneeling to a king. Nowhere were there flowers, fruits, and flowering trees, but supposedly Findhorn was growing them all and more. According to the magazine article, Peter Caddy had labored for years in some endless wasteland of sand and gorse creating a horticultural marvel. To the astonished visitors and neighbors who asked his secret, his answer was simple but cryptic: "Love." Not a startling conclusion in itself, but the results apparently were. I had half-prepared myself for a disappointment, knowing how stories gain currency and strength over large distances. Man is always seeking that upon which he can hang his hat of faith. Was

Findhorn another inflated story? A rumor gestated in the doubts and frustrations of the seventies? It seemed that it might be as I looked out my window and watched the semi-barren crofts.

Having visited top organic farms and gardens throughout America, the past provided vivid pictures of lush growth which contrasted sharply with the harsh environs. Doubts and disbelief began to root and grow. How could the fablelike stories of Findhorn be true? Heading as far north as Juneau, Alaska, every mile took me farther from the possibility, closer to sparse vegetation and dampening spirits. The terrain outside seemingly sealed Findhorn's fate, and an uneasy knowing of having been the fool sent its suckers around my mind and crowded my thoughts. Having traveled across an ocean on the strength of a magazine article and a mimeographed pamphlet, I began to think of excuses to turn back. I had left the United States in brilliant clear summery weather, and here in Scotland it felt as if winter were coming next week. The cold seeped into the carriage, and the chill made me feel that much more uncomfortable with my task.

Darkness was descending. In the distance a large field of stubble had been set ablaze. In the gray mist against the orange fire stood a dark figure, silhouetted with a fork in his hand, staring at the fire. The times were hard: nobody wanted his straw, so he was burning his fields to get rid of it. What was the farmer thinking as he brooded, standing motionless, gazing into his ancestral heritage vanishing into smoke? He stood utterly alone, isolated by his act, pondering his fate as he watched the billowy black clouds rise into the evening gloom. A poor crofter scratching his existence from a rocky hillside, bound by convenience to burn his fields because he was helpless to do anything else, bound by an ancient ignorance and the limitations of his consciousness. What would he think of Devas and Nature Spirits?

As the last carriage passed, he slowly turned toward the

train. His dark eyes were met by mine, weary with travel and doubt. The blackened earth and ritual fire, steaming in the rain, presented a vision of stray elemental forces eating at the earth's vitals, presided over by a pitchforked tiller of the darkness. He disappeared into the gloom as the lights in the carriage were turned on. Our destination of Inverness was announced.

Scotland is dramatically bisected by a major fault starting in the southwest at Loch Linnhe, creating the "rift" of the Great Glen. Through the Glen passes the Caledonian Canal, which finally meets the famous Loch Ness, a narrow 26-mile body of icy waters where prehistoric amphibians are claimed to be sighted disporting off the ruins of Urquhart Castle. The waters of the Loch empty into the River Ness and finally, a few miles downstream, into the Moray Firth at Inverness, the Highland capital of Scotland.

To the southeast of the mouth of the Firth are the Cairngorms, the "blue mountains," solid rocklike boulders around which corries and canyons have been carved which level off into grouse moors and peat-covered heaths. The peaks are bald and bare with only the thinnest cover of bracken and moss, their view usually hidden by masses of clouds formed when the warm air from the south meets the mountain cold.

It is the Kingdom of the Wind. The never ceasing and constant moan and howl speak to some, and those that can hear say that this is where the winds are born. The Kingdom of the Wind is populated by an endless succession of clouds which chart the vast blue lands in mantles of gold, cloaks of gray, and feet of rain. Upon the mountaintops their march is a frozen blast, an icy stamp of supremacy, while in the ravines below, in the thick and heady mists, red deer and rabbits nibble the fresh shoots of heather. The mountains are surrounded by a vast series of dwarf shrub moors, eaten away by the rain, leaving a highly acid peat instead of soil. Lacking oxygen and the ability to support aerobic bacteria, these are largely sterile and infertile; little grows except heathers, crowberries, and occasionally the insectivorous sundews and butterworts.

From the Cairngorms flows the River Nethy to the Spey Valley, where a rich alluvial soil has been laid down over thousands of years, the prosperous farms and fat livestock bearing testimony to the sudden change in the soil. To the east is the Laigh of Moray, some 25 miles along the eastern coast from Inverness, a rich tract of low-lying land composed of a reddish sandstone which produces malting barley for Scotland's distilleries. In the past, when Scotland was in the throes of a famine, the people of the Laigh would put out great kettles of porridge to feed the starving pilgrims. After agricultural bounty had brought prosperity to the region, the village of Findhorn, situated on the tip of a peninsula extending from the Laigh, was transformed from a sleepy village of fishermen to a major port. Boats built in Findhorn of native oak and larch would ply the North Seas laden with malt, salmon, and hides, returning with wine, spices, tobacco, silk, and muslin. The Great Rain of 1829 sent a mammoth torrent of water down the Findhorn River into the Bay of Findhorn, sweeping the village out to sea. It was rebuilt again, but when the railways came, it collapsed as a center of commerce and returned to fishing.

The present village, located some two miles from the original, is built on a sand spit which grows three or four feet per year outward into the Firth because of the sweeping currents of Burghead Bay. On the other side of the village is Findhorn Bay, which is now silted over, in part because of the sloppy agricultural and forestry practices of its highland neighbors. Small sailboats use it in the summer, but the 100-ton schooners of old are merely a dream and a faded photograph in the local pub. It was but a few years ago when around the well-worn benches on the jetty, the air crackled with stories and tales of the last men who had sailed those schooners, reliving their past while occasionally pausing to "flummox" the queries of English tourists in a burr so thick you could stand on it.

The benches are now empty; but near the jetty, the last boat builder still remembers, for his uncle, now over ninety, is the only man alive to have sailed the schooners from the bay. Frank Whyte stubbornly maintains tradition in his unheated shop next to the shore, building small fishing skiffs with native skill and simple tools. He knows he is the last. The young ones have gone off to Glasgow, and times are such that many an afternoon is free and he will gladly share tales of the Firth and the men and boats that once sailed it.

I had hitchhiked that day from Inverness, arriving in the afternoon in the village of Findhorn, not realizing that I had gone past the community of Findhorn, the two being of the same name but separate. I met Frank in front of his shop to ask directions and he pointed back down the road with his pipe. He looked me over and then looked up at the sky.

" 'Tis a storm comin' up surely." Before I knew what hit me, he was talking away, punctuating every other line with bursts of laughter and mirth, eyes a'twinkling and pipe a'wavin' in the air.

"Paul your name, is it? Well, you've come to a fine place, you 'ave. 'Ere 'tis three months of bad weather and nine of wind." He laughed quickly and stole a glance at the sky as if to say he was just kidding. Here was a man whose life's fabric was tightly interwoven with the sky and the wind, and his comment sounded more like a lover's tease than an observation on the weather.

"But do na get me wrong, we're happy and content reared here. My life is the sea, either makin' the boats to put upon it, or in it m'self. America, are you now? 'Tis

9

a big country, I hear. Compared to your country Britain is just a wee isle you can spit across."

He was laughing again. He loved his own jokes best, that was sure.

"During the war, I ken two 'blackies' so big you could take two oars and go to sea in their boots. Aye, must be a mighty big country you 'ave there."

His laughter could now be heard a good block down the road. Frank radiated the vitality of fresh salt air, and when you talked to him it felt like it was blowing in your face.

" 'Tis mostly English we 'ave up here now, talkin' to each other at the Royal Yacht Club like they had hot tatties in their mouths, talkin' 'bout a bloody gale as a 'force four' wind, always checkin' their watches and tables. I've nae use for watches and clocks—'tis whether the tide is going in or out is all that's of interest to me." He leaned a little closer with a puckish grin. "At the club, they put out a lit candle you see, and if it blows out, the wind's too strong to go out, and if it stays lit, there's not enough wind to sail in. I wet my finger and either it's a wee puffie or it's nae blowin'."

A great explosion of mirthful sound and spittle knocked me back a moment.

"My life here is the sea, but I never actually went to sea except for fishin' and sailin'. If I had, which is what I wanted to do, it would be about this time in my life that I would be tiring of it, you know, and I would want to settle down a bit. I would go inland, and do you know how I would know if I was far enough from the sea, Paul? I would bear two oars over my shoulders, and when I got far enough inland that people did na know what they were, then I would know that I was far enough away."

Another great roar of laughter. He looked down the road toward the direction of the Findhorn Community.

"I've spent some time with the folk down the road. They are the greatest people you'll ever meet. They live and let

live, in complete harmony with each other. 'Tis a wee village, you know, and you hear all sorts of stories, a rumor
here, a bit of gossip there, but it's like passin' a tale around
the table. They get twisted around. 'Twas a lady who said
they was a 'shower of weirdies,' and 'tis others who are
afraid, frightened because they seem so well educated,
thinkin' maybe they will find some way of influencin' the
kiddies. They were sayin' there was bathin' in the nude
and all that. Why, for goodness' sakes, I do it m'self sometimes, right off the boat, but I do na do it here off the
blinkin' jetty front of the townfolk, you know, and neither
do they.

"Oh, we heard lots of stories in the beginnin', but less
and less now. I take 'em as I find 'em. You don't go through
life stickin' to what others say. Why there's more skill up
in that tiny spot than the entire distance from here to
Forres. They really know what they are doin', and we get
along well, we do, and that's the most important thing."

Frank Whyte met Peter Caddy fifteen years ago when
Peter was the manager of the Cluny Hill Hotel, the area's
only four-star hotel at the time.

"Sometimes my sailin' parties would take me for a bit
of a wee dram at the Hotel, and he would come out and
greet us. He was a great guy, I thought. Always cheerful
and ready with a good word, you know, seemed to know
everybody by name. Later I heard how he was seein' things
there, flyin' saucers and spaceships. Well, you can't judge
what another man sees. I have spent nights on the Firth
when it was black as the waistcoat of the Earl of Hell, and
I 'ave seen things that I 'ave no ken for. Many things 'ave
I seen out there that I can't explain, so maybe I know what
he was talkin' about, and maybe I don'."

Frank had been right about the storm, for in the time
we talked, the sky completely clouded over and a cold rain
started to blow in from the southwest. I left him with his
pipe in one hand and a chisel in the other and began to

walk down the road along the Bay toward the Findhorn Bay Caravan Park.

From Frank's comments and some stories I had heard in London, it began to dawn on me that Findhorn was not just a few people isolated on a sand dune, but a large and multifaceted community with religious overtones. Frank never mentioned the gardens at all, although he did talk about their skill in building and carpentry, something nearer to his heart. Despite his warm endorsement, there was a strange feeling about Findhorn that I received from him, as well as others in the village. When the name Findhorn Community was brought up, there was a change in attitude, a sort of blank and uncomprehending look on faces, an expression of withdrawal. It was not a subject that most people cared to discuss, but those who would spoke darkly of that "Caddy chap," with 'is wives and cars, getting the bounce from his hotel for raidin' the tills and takin' money from the young 'uns. But Frank was the only person who actually had met and visited with the community. The others were a suspicious and grumbly lot, afraid to go near the place.

As I walked away from the village, I saw to my left a large moorland comprised of shingle and sand dunes, spotted with furze and broom, appearing forsaken and lifeless. On the right was Findhorn Bay, a great expanse of mud and drying seaweed at low tide. Straight ahead, past the Findhorn Community, was the Kinloss Royal Air Force Base, where large planes were descending out of the overcast. On the fourth side of the Caravan Park was a bomb and torpedo dump, surrounded by barbed-wire-topped chainlink fences, patrolled by Alsatian guard dogs and Land-Rovers bristling with rifle barrels. Hardly a garden spot, it seemed the last place to start a "New Age" community. What I had seen from the train seemed paradisiacal in comparison, for here it looked as if an incendiary bomb had devastated the place some years back and it was only now coming to life again.

A passing motorist rescued me from the rain and deposited me in front of the Caravan Park, a conglomeration of new and old mobile homes and trailers parked three deep down the length of an abandoned aircraft pan. I entered a door to the Caravan Park Office, where three rather dour and officious men stared at me, wet and dripping. I was looking for Peter Caddy, I said, hoping that none of them were he. One of them silently motioned next door to a grocery store. Behind the counter was a wispy girl, obviously American, who pointed to a bungalow at the intersection of the main road and a smaller tarmac one 50 yards away. She said she would phone Peter and tell him I was on my way up.

The rain had stopped, and I walked slowly, trying to catch a glimpse of something that fitted the descriptions of Findhorn Gardens, seeing nothing to my right except trailers parked on the grass. As I approached the intersection, there came wheeling around the corner of the cedarwood bungalow a large, squarely built man in his midfifties. He was wearing a huge white bulky sweater from which a balding and beaming russet-colored head emerged, looking somewhat like a giant beetroot. In his khaki pants and black shoes, he seemed to represent the ultimate figure of authority, embodying every principal, scoutmaster, dean of men, and policeman I had ever met. He radiated an absolute sense of authority and control, and his voice booming out to greet me did nothing to lessen that impression. Here was a man who seemed to have complete mastery over his destiny, as if every detail in his life was working out exactly as planned, and in that moment I felt as if I was one of those details. There was hardly a hair out of place on his head, and one immediately suspected that no hairs were out of place in his life either. Somehow, the idea of a sensitive gardener working closely with plants and nature spirits seemed completely incongruous. I don't know what I expected, but Peter Caddy no more evoked the image of a gardener than did General Patton. Walking, or rather striding, around with him to his bungalow, I caught a first glimpse of the garden. The sun had just peeked out for a moment, and there leaning over the roadway were great banks of red, orange, and yellow roses, a strange thing indeed to be growing in the sand.

If Peter was General Patton, his wife Eileen was something between Spring Byington and "Happy" Rockefeller. She was waiting for us, kettle in hand, to brew a cup of tea. She cheerfully moved through the cramped quarters with grace and precision, calmly asking about the trip up while she efficiently arranged the cups and cookies and placed the tea cozy over the pot. I had read in "The Findhorn Garden" that the whole of the community was run and based on guidance which she received from "God" but as with her husband, I had difficulty visualizing her role in the community. Smaller, yet equally as strong as her husband, she appeared to be more like my silver-haired aunt from Bethesda than a mystic who spoke to God.

"Why are you here?" Peter wanted to know. He took a great gulp of tea and waited for an answer.

I reiterated the reasons given in an earlier letter to him, that I was interested in alternative agriculture and there was a possibility of doing an article for an American publication.

He nodded quickly in a no-nonsense way, as if it were perfectly normal for people to come 4,000 miles to see him, popped a Yorkshire Parkin in his mouth, chewed it, swallowed another gulp of tea, and said: "What do you want to know?"

His bluntness was uncompromising and slightly unnerving. I can't remember what I said, but I stammered out something about life on the planet and consciousness. Whatever it was, I don't think he was very impressed, for in the next moment he was getting up, asking me to follow so that my lodging could be arranged. Explaining that because of a conference and the Festival of Michaelmas there was little space, he introduced me to the "accommodations focalizer" and bade good day.

The "accommodations focalizer" was a well-scrubbed, rosy-cheeked Swedish girl who spoke a thick but precisely accented English. Alice was in a dither, a slightly detuned Mad Hatter who let everyone know she was "awfully busy." Leading me across the road to another bungalow called the "Universal Foundation," which is owned in absentia by the former White Rajah of Sarawak, she produced a small map on which she circled a black rectangle numbered 117 which was a few hundred yards from where we were standing. This was my caravan, soap and towels were there, milk and cornflakes were available in the community center, and with that she left.

The area to which I was directed was called Pineridge, the overflow from the burgeoning community. Sites had been created only recently for caravans, but very little work had gone into the area because the land was being rented from month to month. If it was rather bleak and unadorned horticulturally speaking, it at least gave one the sense of what Findhorn must have been like in the original days. There was hardly anything growing except some gorse and ling heather, and they weren't doing so well at that. At the far end of this expanse of sand was an elderly 8-by-20-foot metal box on wheels, its blue paint peeling and dropping onto the sand. Number 117 was parked at the end of a dirt road along a barbed wire fence on the other side of which grew a fledgling tree plantation of lodge pole pine. To the right was a galvanized coal bin, and farther over was another metal box on wheels, same construction, different color.

In all fairness, it was one of the most depressing and dreary sights I had ever seen. It seemed like a dreadful place to stay even for one night, but the idea of living there was appalling. Stepping inside was no relief, for there was a great clutter in the room: esoteric and spiritual books were strewn about; posters, flyers, leaflets, and a healthy assortment of subcultural artifacts were lying in complete disarray. The fact that it had no heat except a small electric "fire" was hardly improved by the fact that the small port-hole windows would not completely shut. I remembered reading tales of Tibetan youth seeking admission to monasteries having to wait silently outside the gates with their begging bowl in the freezing weather in order that their sincerity be tested, but I didn't want to join or be tested. I simply wanted to see the garden. The wind was starting to blow in gusts around and through the curtains, and I felt cold and stupid. What madness had brought me here? I had come all the way to Britain but, seeing no reason to waste my time here, determined to cut my stay to two days instead of the week originally planned.

Since there was an hour before dinner, I left the caravan and, finding a small path, began to walk the mile toward the beach. In Scotland the wind was becoming a companion, an element of constancy I began to accept, and it now blew harder than ever before. Rabbits darted across the path into round openings in the clumps of gorse. One pebbled ridge after another indicated that I was walking on what had recently been beach. On the leeward side of the last ridge before the beach were clumps of marram and couch grass half-covered by the shifting sands, while between the dunes in small depressions were carpets of a thick spongy grass dotted with a blackened dwarf heather.

Climbing over the last sand dune, I was hit by a furious force which whipped my parka and slapped the hood flap rapidly against my back. The water was pounding into a row of concrete tank blocks and bunkers, war relics placed there to protect the Air Force base from invasion. Eaten and eroded by the tide and wind, they lined the beach in both directions for miles, a disarrayed clutter of old paranoia crumbling into the sea.

Looking across the dark gray water to the Mountain of

Morven silhouetted across the Firth, I felt the real primitiveness of Scotland. Having traveled along roads and rails, I had seen the thin veneer of prosperity which had only recently come to the north, eclipsing a long history of toil and hunger. Scotland was a country where "savage streams tumble over savage mountains" and where the milk ran so thin that live frogs were added to churns to make an oily soup called butter. Like the peat cutters of the western isles who lived in shielings of furze and heather and ate one meal a day of bannocks, sloke, and potatoes, those who lived between the sea and the rocks and peopled the Kingdom of the Wind had never known a life of ease.

The wind shifted, and huge anvil-headed clouds, aglow and fiery in the setting sun, thick as starch and massive as mountains, moved across the sky, dropping sheets of rain to the northwest. The skyscape, far more impressive than the surrounding landscape, was a vast golden plain from which supernatural buttermilk mountains, defying gravity, rose and curled into the waning sun. In the netherland of no sun and no night, the golds and silvers of the horizon slowly transmuted to magentas and purples, a mauve twilight world on which one last cloud caught the light of the dying day. High above and independent of the other clouds, it was heading for shore when it was blotted out by sundeath and blown into the windy grayness.

I slowly walked back to the trailer park.

The Buzz and the Glow

Great Lord of Mercy!!! The End of the World!!!

A great red gouge rips into my stunned and shrieking cortex! There are howling hurricanes in my ears.

"It's DOOM!" I say, leaping out of my sleeping bag to a sunny morning takeoff of a Vulcan bomber winding up its engines a mile across Johnny Bichan's barley field. It is a gut-rending, titanium steel wail, a thunderous fiery-hot plasmic sound which singes my brain and leaves it like a burned bannock cake, smoking and carbonized.

Good frosty Findhorn morning! Royal Air Force reveille —two minutes of complete mental obliteration. I look at my watch. It is 7:53, just enough time for tea, toast, and Sanctuary.

My roommate is already up. An American from London, he is carefully rolling Golden Virginia tobacco in Rizla Green, tamping down the ends with wooden matches, looking down the sides like a gun barrel, and then laying them aside neat as chalksticks. He glances over out of the corner of his eye to where I am standing and then carefully unfolds another paper.

"Good mornin' to ya', brothah! Wasn't that some bird?" Golden doesn't look up from his work but continues: "'Bout blew me 'way. Didn't know they had big birds around here too." He softly chuckles at his own joke, like if that was a big bird, just wait until you see the plants growing in the garden.

My Golden Virginian makes the tea and toast while I splash cold brown water on my face.

"These cats really have a scene goin' on up heah. You figure it out?" Golden turns to me with his slitty blue eyes, squinting into a nonexistent sun and remembers I just appeared the night before, which pretty much answers the question. I don't know nothing, just like Golden.

We sit down to a breakfast of brown bread, heather honey, and camomile tea. Golden is talking about something, but my mind drifts back to the previous night, to dinner in the Community Center.

I had met Craig Gibsone, an "Aussie" who is one of the longer residents. He had explained much over dinner that clarified the physical surroundings of Findhorn. According to Craig, Findhorn had started as just one caravan on a rented site of a trailer park, or caravan park as it is called in Britain. It was situated near the rubbish dump and consequently quite isolated from the rest of the caravans. Findhorn had grown from that one caravan, adding more year by year, until now it consisted of forty caravans and fourteen bungalows housing one hundred and thirty members and forty guests. The community owned some of the caravans and bungalows, but most were owned by individuals. There didn't seem to be any concern about ownership one way or the other here. It was a refreshing change from communes I had visited in America where one was required to sign over the whole of one's material possessions before being accepted as a member. There, material possessions were seen as a "hang-up" of which the commune would gladly relieve the individual. But it usually worked out that the "hang-up" of materiality was simply transferred to the greater whole, since it was actually embodied within the person, not the goods or money. At

Findhorn, the emphasis is on the consciousness of the person desiring membership, material contribution above monthly expenses not being a factor.

Nevertheless, it amazed me that the community was built and was building on leased land—short leases at that! The gardens, the bungalows, the Sanctuary, and the newly built Community Center where we were eating were built on land Findhorn did not own. Was this faith or stupidity I wanted to know but didn't ask. Pineridge was not even leased, although they were trying, so far unsuccessfully, to negotiate a lease for it. Land simply wasn't for sale here. Everyone was holding on to land for dear life because of the North Sea oil boom that was expected to hit the area, and the scraps of land that were for sale were going for an astronomical $20,000 per acre. Twenty grand for sand and pebbles.

I asked why the community didn't move to another spot, one more favorable to its development. Craig replied that Findhorn was located on a power point, a "cosmic" power point, and that a great deal of energy was focused at Findhorn. I thought that to be a rather obscure and glib statement, but the thought had hardly gone out of my head into the ether before I noticed something "strange" about the dining room. At first it had looked like one big happy family gobbling dinner at a ski lodge. There were eighty or ninety people in attendance that night. The lighting was golden amber and reflected beautifully off the ash tables and cork-colored tiles. But in the next moment the whole room began to "buzz." The Buzz was not a noise but a vibration that permeated the room. It was felt in between the sentences, murmurs, and drifting laughter of adjoining conversations. The feeling became stronger and stronger. I looked up and met the intense and directed blue gaze of Alexis, a forty-year-old ex-actor from New York who had been studying astrology for the past five years at Findhorn. He was looking at me quite fixedly and then looked back again to his meal of vegetarian shepherd's pie. It was as if he had read my mind and was silently saying: *Now do you feel it? It is not the gardens or the buildings or even the words we speak. It is this. Do you feel it now? This is what we are really talking about.* I looked over to Craig, and he gave me a look identical to Alexis's. Jesus! I looked down at my shepherd's pie and felt a little shaky about it all.

Something was happening all right, and I was the Mr. Jones, and I really didn't know what it was. Evans-Wentz talks about Carnac in his *Fairy Faith in Celtic Countries*: ". . . there seem to be certain favoured places on the earth where its magnetic and even more subtle forces are most powerful and most easily felt by persons susceptible to such things. . . ." I looked about me once again, and it seemed that every one of my fellow diners had the same intensity of Alexis and Craig, and what's more, they all *glowed*. Yet, that "glow" was the only common and unifying factor that I could discern. A more heterogeneous group of people living together in a community I could not have imagined.

There were matronly types stiffly dressed in starchy linen dresses and chiffon shawls with brown squarish pumps that squeaked when they walked across the floor, reminding me of the women you would see in the front row of Boston Theosophical meetings.

Thirty or forty Americans were in the room, most between the ages of twenty and thirty, slightly louder in voice and dress than the remaining diners. Most were what are commonly called freaks. They had dropped out of something, even out of being freaks. What gave them the Glow was their utter cleanliness of mind and body. Freaks, yes, but without the underground flotsam of torn clothes, matted hair, and decaying faces. Everyone just sparkled.

Craig pointed to one table where an extremely animated conversation was being carried out in both German and

English. There sat the painter Mary Bauermeister Stock-hausen, the wife of the composer Karl heinz Stockhausen, with a German peasant clairvoyant named Joseph Giebel. She was the interpreter to the rest of the table, which included an American doctor, Jeff, a Jewish Yoga instructor from Los Angeles named Ganga with his wife Radha, and a stunningly beautiful English writer, Jill Purce, who definitely had the Glow. The whole of the group had arrived from Germany to attend a conference entitled "Education in the New Age."

In a remotely located "New Age" community that specialized in contact with plants through the invisible Kingdoms, I would have expected to have found a rather narrow and equally specialized spectrum of humanity. Yet everywhere I looked there was another type of person, so that I soon had to forget about types altogether. Typecasting did not explain why they were here. It underlined the fact that Findhorn had an attraction that cut right across age, nationality, and social class. The only thing in common was the Glow, and in the morning what I remembered most clearly about the previous night was that Glow—and the Buzz.

Golden lit up one of his fat Golden Virginias, and clouds of blue smoke filled the tiny room. Outside the window a steamy mist was rising from the sunny patches of sand while frost still lay in the shade. There was the faint smell of coal smoke as the assorted collection of trailers, mobile homes, caravans, and bungalows came to life. In the morning sunshine, it rather appeared as a refugee camp or a Hoovertown that had taken root and sprouted. Wooden annexes were built onto trailers which, with flattened tires and rusted axles, would never see the road again. It was an old-age home for elderly caravans. Each one seemed cared for and freshly painted. Everyone was making the best of it. If my immediate surroundings had earlier given me cause for gloom, it didn't seem to bother the residents at all.

Golden began talking about how the women here were "mighty fine and proud," another of his cowboy-from-New-Jersey observations about Findhorn. He was staring fixedly over my shoulder out the window. I turned to see what had caught his attention. Next door windows were opening, curtains were blowing in the morning sea breezes, and a large and luxuriant blonde moved between her two rooms, sweeping, dusting, and singing. Golden sighed, looked back into the room and then at his lap.

There in his hands was a book: *Revelation: The Birth of a New Age*. He ran the tip of his tobacco-stained thumb across the pages, making a sound like the hesitant rasp of an insect. While he fanned the pages he seemed momentarily lost in reverie, the quietest he had been all morning. He finally looked up.

"You know, I asked someone here which book I should read to understand Findhorn, and this is what they gave me: *Revelation*, by David Spangler. Written by a kid, I heard. This is one heavy book, yeahhh. I jus' can't read no moh than one page at a time. No, sir, this is some heavy stuff." And he seemed to drop back into an undirected but thought-filled silence.

I had tried to read the same book the night before without much more success. I realized that by the time I was twenty pages into it I didn't remember a word I had read past the first two. Supposedly, David Spangler receives messages from a presence called "Limitless Love and Truth" and records the words. The book was a commentary on transmissions received in 1970. What I remembered from the book was a Christopher Fry quotation in the foreword: "Affairs are now soul size./The enterprise/Is exploration into God. . . ."

"Well, 'bout time we make it on over to Sanctuary, I reckon," drawls Golden, and off we go.

As we step out of our metal icebox, that large beaming blonde in the next caravan drops her broom, grabs her jacket, and runs to join us. She pounces on Golden with a big hug, and then puts one warm arm about each of us, and away we go down the pebbled road to the main community. Joy! Joy Drake sidles up in a big thick woolen coat collared to her ears, her enormous sparkling eyes just barely showing beneath four-inch bangs. She gives us all a hearty "good morning" in the most proper of English, and the four of us are now linked arm in arm, walking in step to the Sanctuary. And then Sarah, Sarah, silver-haired sheepish Sarah, comes out of her caravan, wagging her body like a puppy dog just given a sausage, and joins us around the Pineridge turn. We're onto the macadam now, and Don Zontine, a fullback-broad, mustachioed, and bearded Italian-American, throws a glorious Tom Bombadillian laugh carelessly into the crackling morning air. And right behind Don, the short and spectacled Hans Poulsen animatedly hobbles up in his black boots and furry flight jacket, stops in front of the six, does a quick jig under his brightly colored granny-square cap, gives an exaggerated stage wink, and in a thick Australian accent says, "Hiya, Cobbers." And now we are seven, laughing and giggling, walking through and over potholes, puddles, and pebbles past Elsie's, the Hiltons', the pottin' shed, the Park. . . .

"ssssHHHHH!!!" Joy gives us the word with a short stubby finger across her puckered ruby lips, and stifled giggles signal that the morning march is over. We file singly into a small room, shed our coats and shoes, and enter a larger room where there are about sixty-five upholstered chairs arranged in two concentric circles. People pour in until all the chairs are full and then begin sitting in the open space in the middle of the floor.

To one side Eileen Caddy sits sentinel still, 100-watt connection plugged in, radiating light from every silvery filament of hair, clear out of the Sanctuary into space, and it's a wonder her chair doesn't go up in smoke.

Peter tiptoes in over the bodies, glances first at his watch and then at the twelve-dozen lidded eyeballs, a zonked collection of teenagers, grandmothers, bushy beards, bald heads, and beatific ladies from ten countries facing some invisible point in the middle of the room. PLOP! Peter sits down, shuffles a few papers, and then all you can hear are the sparrows cutting loose in the gorse bushes outside the window.

Communion.

Calm union.

The morning fabric.

Eileen the spinner, Peter the weaver, the warp and woof, the listener and the server, contemplation and action. Eileen has been sitting there for two hours, and Peter looks as if it is all he can do to sit in his chair for ten minutes. His eyelids are quivering he is so anxious to get on with the day. The minds and spirits of the community are overlapping in and around and out, every soul threading its way into a delicate etheric mesh. There is utter silence.

Slowly the murmurous and bewitching vibrato of Jenny Walker rolls out. Seventy-nine years of prayer and reverence speak in vibrations so distinct that each syllable sounds like five. It is a voice so liltingly Scottish that one feels as if a peat-stained mountain burn is pouring into the room.

OWWW-UUR-R FAAA-THER-R-R. . . . There is a pause that seems infinite. The mind, startled at the intrusion of this powerful voice, reels at the subsequent silence, breaks anchor, and begins to float away with the receding sound. . . . WHOOO AR-R-RT IN HEAA-VENN. . . . Heaven, right in this room. The Buzz and the Magic are thick as pudding. Get ready, this is going to be like no Lord's Prayer you have ever heard. . . . HAL-LOW-ED BE THY NAME. . . . "Affairs are now soul size." Warm waves of peace, calm, and serenity wash over silvery spines. Layer after layer of new meaning is gently revealed by this pulsating voice. . . . THY KINGDOM COME. . . . The power is growing, every tuner has got the same band now, the signal is strong, consciousness is arranged throughout the room like a perfect pattern of iron filings gathered about this oral magnet. . . . THY . . . WILL . . . BE . . . DONE. . . . Oneness, we know each other better now, better than we ever have, right now! Jenny's voice is throbbing. . . . ON . . . EARTH. . . . Earth? Back to Earth! That small bluish orb over there! Spaceship Sanctuary calling Earth, do you read me, Earth? . . . AS IT IS IN HEA-VEN. . . . "Know that when you learn to lose yourself, you will reach the Beloved. There is no secret to be learned, and more than this is not known to me. . . ." Gone. . . . The whole room is gone . . . the prayer becomes a mantric intercession into space . . . reverberating . . . on . . . and . . . on . . . second . . . after . . . second . . . minute . . . after . . . minute . . . into . . . the . . . silent . . . golden . . . warmth. . . .

"There will be a lecture on tape by David Spangler for visitors today at five o'clock in the Universal Foundation bungalow."

We've landed.

Sanctuary is over, punctuated by Peter's short announcement. People file out to find their shoes in the vestibule. They are smiling, rosy, and happy. With moist eyes, they squeeze hands and generally act as if they hadn't seen each other for a month. There is a joy about to burst through the community and set it spinning and weaving.

Peter stands outside reeling off five-second conversations with a dozen people, setting the whole in motion, making last-minute adjustments, sharing bits of thought and ideas he may have had in Sanctuary, whispering to his drivers just before the race. . . . They're off!!! Fourteen gardeners, six office workers, a clutch of typists, seven carpenters, ten cooks, a pair of plumbers, four weavers, five printers, three candlemakers, two soundmen, six shopkeepers, twelve actors and actresses, and a prophet.

From the greater attunement of the Sanctuary, each in-

dividual goes to his or her department for a group attunement. In each of the eighteen departments, everyone holds
hands and meditates for a moment on the vision of the
group, its purpose, role, and function within the greater
whole, and then the day's work begins.

After Sanctuary I wandered around the community and
the garden, watching the activity. Peter caught up with me
and reminded me not to miss the ten o'clock tour he
was giving. I stopped to talk with Leonard, one of
the gardeners, who was watering a bed of flowers. We
walked around the garden together, he answering questions
while I took notes on the names and varieties of flowers.
He spoke softly in a thick Lancashire accent and was conversant with every plant name, common and Latin, and
demonstrated a profound knowledge of gardening. The
paths along which we walked were lined with marigolds,
alyssum, lobelias, pansies, nemesia, woolly apple mint, and
columbine. In the beds were thick and profuse clumps
of flowers, brightly competing with one another in the
morning sun: petunias, silver dust, asters, Michaelmas and
Livingstone daisies, poppies, campanula, fuchsia, delphinium, clarkia, helichrysum, monkshood, cosmos, ajuga,
echium, and many others. It was an amazing display, and
every flower seemed perfectly in bloom on this crisp late
September day.

We eventually met up with Mathew, the head gardener.
Peter no longer works in the garden, his duties as "custodian" of the community having completely preempted his
time. He has turned the job over to several gardeners from
Blackpool known around the community as the "gnomes."
All of them were formerly apprentice gardeners and have
combined much of the orthodoxy they learned with the
lessons that Peter absorbed in his eight years as gardener.
They have continued Peter's work, and the garden has
expanded, but many of the phenomenal aspects of the
garden disappeared when they took over. There are still

some unusually large plants here and there, but since Peter left the garden it has become more "normal" in respect to the size and proportion of the plants.

I asked Mathew why the plants were more normal now.

"The growth here was fantastic to demonstrate to Peter Caddy and to others that it was possible. Now we know it is possible to work with the Nature Kingdom, but we no longer have the need to produce a plant where it won't normally grow. Just because some of these plants were growing in the middle of the cold in the dry sand didn't mean that they were happy about it. They were there to show the power and potential of cooperation. But still, without even pushin' we have some tremendous things this year. The roses are enormous, don't know what got into them, and there are some amazingly big things in other areas. But if you show somebody a forty-pound cabbage, they get hung up in the forty-pound-cabbage trip and think only in terms of size, form, and quantity. They take for granted the being and consciousness behind that cabbage. Instead, all they see is the size, not the beauty and perfection of it."

I must admit, I had hoped to see one of those cabbages.

Nevertheless, the garden is still astonishing to my eyes. I have never seen anything like it in my life. There is richness of color and variety everywhere you look. Each plant seems to be in perfect condition. Weeds are hardly to be seen, but then there is hardly any room for them, the garden being so thick and profuse. It is the last week in September, and the flowers are neon bright at latitudes farther north than Moscow and parts of Alaska. Roses are in full bloom over the roadways, cosmos plants stand six feet in the air, and bumble bees, drunk from nectar, stagger around the purple sedum. It is an orgy in the plant kingdom. Two hundred feet away, the thorny furze and broom are sending out their ropy fibrous roots in search of water and nutrients. Here in the garden, the flowers are oversized, brilliant, and turgid with moisture and juices. The trees are erect and strong despite being rooted in soft sand and blown about by 60-mile-an-hour winds. They include native larch, spruce, and pine, but also dogwood, hawthorn, laburnum, eucalyptus, mountain ash, poplar, and silver birch. Behind the beds of flowers and amid the trees are shrubs including hypericum, honeysuckle, witch hazel, weigela, buddleia, lilacs, climbing roses, holly, viburnum, snowberry tamarisk, dwarf heathers and conifers, and others.

When I first saw the gardens the riot of color overwhelmed my senses. But time allows the eye to rove around and inspect it more carefully. Everywhere I put my hand into the soil there was sand two or three inches under the compost. It is like gardening on a beach. Yet staring at you and waving brightly in the sun is a compact bunch of healthy flowers. It defies rational analysis, and so far, no scientific authority has been able to explain the phenomenon of Findhorn.

I asked Mathew and Leonard about Nature Spirits and whether in "working" with them they actually perceived them. Both said that they did not perceive them directly, but both felt that they were intuitively guided by the Nature Spirits. Leonard told the story of how he went to several deeply rooted bushes a few days before they had to be removed and quietly told them when and why they had to be moved. When the day came to remove them they could be easily pulled out of the ground with one hand as if they had completely released their "hold" on life. For comparison, Leonard went to one of the bushes that was not to be taken out and pulled on it. It wouldn't budge.

We were sitting in the Rockery, built around a lily pond in front of the "college" building. The sunny day had produced a strong wind from the southwest. Between pauses in his thoughts the head Gnome leaned down and put a bit of sweet thyme in his mouth. It was just the tiniest little plant growing between the cracks in the foot-path. But it was no accident; Mathew had planted it in the spring and had watched it thrive there. He spoke quietly of Pan.

"Pan is the body within every life force, everything that procreates, everything that dies, everything that moves. Pan, as popularly understood, is a distortion, just like Jesus is. People put Jesus on a cross and keep him there. And people put Pan to hoof and horn. But to me, Pan is a bit like lace curtains and glistening gossamers, little grasses and ferns, mosses growing in between the cracks. This little piece of thyme down here that I am taking bites of is every bit of Pan. Pan is the little worm crawling along the sand in the bottom of the sea, and he is the great blue whale that comes along and eats it. Pan is so vast and so dynamic, yet so sincere and gentle. . . . Didn't Wordsworth write about it when he said: 'Ten thousand saw I at a glance . . .'? People have been attuned to Pan for a millennium. They may not have known it, but I am sure those painters who painted these woodland scenes were unknowingly kicked in their arse by Pan. How else can you explain it?"

I couldn't stay to ponder that question. It was five before ten, and I had to get to the Community Center before the tour started. The one thing that Peter emphasized was Punctuality. At Findhorn it came right under Godliness and Cleanliness in priority and was expressed in the oft-repeated phrase: "Being attuned is being in the right place, doing the right thing, at the right *time!*"

"Oh yeahh, isn't that beautiful." Shoshana is standing in the hall of the Community Center, head cocked against the wall, clasping the morning's mail to her bosom with both arms. She has a huge pixie grin on a Siamese cat face. Almond-eyed, lithe and graceful, she lets forth another "Oh, beautiful" every fifteen seconds to a girl who is telling Shoshana about a dream she had the night before.

"Wow! It sounds like you really got there." She is dressed in an outrageous magenta poncho with her long brown hair sprayed about the opening.

"That's just too much," she exclaims.

The whole community seems to run effortlessly; people glide in and out of buildings, waving and smiling to each other, stopping sometimes to have a word or two.

"Isn't that incredible! Woww!" Shoshana is shaking her head in disbelief.

The conversations I hear are not the frenzied oral memos passed from one department to another, but usually dreams, visions, or inspired thoughts.

"I can really dig it, yeahh." She is nodding her head enthusiastically up and down in agreement now.

There seem to be two levels of communication going on at once. The daily operative messages like we need a screwdriver or new water pump are neatly fitted in the cracks of conversations about spirits, plants, weather, people, or anything that prompts one to converse.

"Woww. It really sounds like you have reached another level!" Shoshana is grinning so broadly that her eyes are narrow little slits.

And yet the community is spotlessly clean. Every caravan or bungalow is immaculately maintained. The "work program" produces excellent results with no hustle and bustle, no obvious signs of work being done.

How can Shoshana do it? She just stands there nodding her head in the middle of the morning, looking absurdly happy, and so does everyone else. Who does the work? Where does it all come from?

"I had asked for a year for a greenhouse; I knew we were to have a greenhouse; Eileen had received positive guidance we were to have a greenhouse, and I just couldn't understand why we didn't have a greenhouse!"

The ten o'clock tour. Peter was pointing to *the* greenhouse, now several years old, next to the Sanctuary. *He* just couldn't understand it! *He* had asked for it, and it didn't come! Some of the people are looking at Peter as if he is an idiot. *What do you expect? You don't get things by just asking for them. You've got to go out and work for. . . .*

"And then I suddenly realized what the problem was. I had been too vague. I came here, measured the space, and asked for an eight-by-twelve-foot cedarwood greenhouse. It came the next week!"

The group of visitors are sure of it now. He is an idiot. They are staring at Peter with equal parts of disbelief, wonder, and astonishment. Just how would an 8-by-12 cedarwood greenhouse show up? It is certainly not something you find lying around in trash heaps.

"This whole community is based on the Law of Manifestation! It depends and runs on its principles. It operates in complete faith that all of our needs will be perfectly met!"

"What if you ask for some article and it does not appear?" A pale, horn-rimmed scholar is obviously enjoying the absurdity of Peter's statement and is now slowly baiting him in perfect Oxford English.

"It always does!" comes the instant response. Peter looks at him for any more questions, as if that question was completely and fully answered.

"Yes, quite, quite! But what if it does not come?" is the reply. The amused scholar is trying to be most tolerant, and he pronounces each word precisely and clearly to Peter. All eyes turn back to Peter.

Peter looks puzzled for a moment. Because of his training in "positive thinking," Peter never uses the word "if" in his speech. It has no meaning for him, having atrophied from his vocabulary years ago. He has difficulty understanding it when someone else uses it. It is *"when,"* not *"if"*— "when it will manifest," not "if it will manifest." "If" is negative thinking, self-defeating, demoralizing, and useless.

In short, it is banished. Just four rules at Findhorn: no dope, no smoking in public areas, a rule can be made by Peter at any time, and no negative thinking! Please! Go to town when you think that way, but not here!

"All our needs are always met. It has never happened," Peter flatly states.

Scholar cannot believe it. He looks at Peter as being totally obtuse, illogical, and preposterous. Scholar is not talking about what was, but about what might be. Scholar sees Peter as a simpleton. There is a total look of exasperation on his face which is quickly replaced by a look of smiling tolerance.

"No, you don't understand, my dear chap. I would have you consider the possibility of some future time or date, when, say, you ask for a motorcar or electric lamp, and it does not 'manifest,' as you so aptly put it!"

Peter glances quickly at the rest of us, a look of total bewilderment and questioning on his face. He wants to know if this guy is serious, and he sees from our faces that he most certainly is.

Peter turns back to Scholar with a large toothy grin, beaming down upon him like a lighthouse to illuminate this darkened little ectomorph, beaming light right down to the pits of Scholar's pupils, and says: "It never happens!"

Peter is still staring at Scholar, his whole face saying one thing—NOW! Don't live in the future, don't live in the past, they don't exist. Live in the presence of God, right now, not a minute from now, not five seconds from now, NOW!

Peter has got all the juice, and Scholar just stands slack-jawed and fidgety at all this raw energy pouring into him, and he knows he has lost the battle because Peter wasn't even fighting.

Some of the others are convinced now. After all, the whole morning had been spent seeing one cedarwood bungalow after another, print shops, darkrooms, studios, a pottery, a shop, a dining room, a college building, and the Community Center, and every one carried at least one tale of "manifestation." Peter has not "worked" for anything that has been received. When Findhorn began, the government gave him eight pounds a week of welfare money. All the rest, according to Peter, came from God. He hasn't had a job for eleven years since he left the nearby Cluny Hill Hotel in 1962. Peter has spent these years enacting the principles of the Law of Manifestation, following Eileen's guidance step by step, in complete and childlike trust right up to this toothy grinning moment in the pits of Scholar's pupils—and now Scholar knows it too!

Life at Findhorn calls for a surrender which is at once frightening and ecstatic. According to Peter, to live at Findhorn one must give up one's own will in favor of a greater will, one which we suppress but one which, when obeyed, will take care of our every need. A "need" means just that, and Peter illustrates this point with stories of the past when Eileen, he, and the three children ate nothing but potato soups and overripe bananas. They stayed alive, their needs were met, and they learned just how few needs they truly had.

The faith that Peter feels is immovable—it is like a rock, as Scholar found out. It doesn't take into consideration logic, intellect, or reason. It is pure faith. The absoluteness of such faith can clash dramatically when it meets the "faithless" who stalk the earth. Bible-toting Christians with pension plans and life insurance are shocked at the absolutes of Findhorn. Freaks and hippies coming to Findhorn expecting a place to "crash" have been directed to the Bed and Breakfast down the road. This is not a community where itinerants can wander in and by their very presence claim "rights." There are no minority rights here. There is no minority "view" here, for there is no minority here. There is no majority either. There are not two sides to an argument because there are no arguments. What sounds wonderful to some may sound weird to others. The major decisions are not made by reason, discussion, or committees. They are made by guidance, sometimes Eileen's, sometimes Peter's in the form of intuition, and sometimes by others.

There are no fixed regulations, there are no orders, there are no chains of command imposed from without. There is only the consciousness of the group constantly striving to maintain and increase their awareness of the God within and demonstrate it in their daily lives. So there is no knowing how something will come to the community, and the corollary to that is that there is no planning for the future. There is only the faith that, in time, all needs will be met, and up to now they have been met 100 percent and there does not seem to be any sign of letting up.

The Law of Manifestation functions like prayer in reverse. Nothing is simply asked for. First the Caddys are told that they are to receive something, usually through Peter's intuition or Eileen's guidance. They then "ask" for it by "holding it in the Light."

From an aluminum caravan set astride a trash dump eleven years ago to the abundant and prosperous community of 130 today lay a thousand incidents of "manifestation" which Peter will gladly and joyfully recount by the hour.

Interestingly, during the tour, Peter only casually mentioned the gardens. Instead he pointed out material objects that had been manifested along the way: a caravan, a garage, some curtains, a bungalow, or a printing press, all of which can be bought, all completely mundane and everyday. Peter would talk on about how they appeared "miraculously," while behind him is a garden which is "miraculous," a garden which people from all over the world have come to see. But Peter takes it in his stride. He seems more fascinated with structures, buildings, and forms.

After touring the whole of the community, Peter invited me to his bungalow for coffee. Eileen was waiting as before, with an iron in one hand and a boiling kettle in the other.

The Caddy living room is a middle-class pastiche of floral carpets, stuffed chairs, a color TV, a mantel clock over a coal fire, a writing desk, and in the middle of their living room, a circular coffee table littered with what appears to be two weeks' worth of correspondence directed to Peter. He informed me that it was only a couple of days' worth.

"Do you think I was too hard on him?" Peter was asking about Scholar and then began to answer his own question.

"It's very important that people know the significance of Findhorn. Here we are actually demonstrating God's plan in concrete ways. We are not just talking a lot of airy fairy stuff about His greatness and how you should live in faith. We are embodying it! We are living it! It's very important that people see that this works, that all of man's needs can be met if he is willing to surrender his life to God. Look at the garden. We didn't say anything about Devas, elves, or Pan for years. We just kept it to ourselves because we knew people couldn't understand it until it had been demonstrated. Only after years of results, and after experts from around the world confirmed the results, could we say to the world: This is how we did it!"

Eileen poured Peter a steaming mug of half coffee and half boiled milk.

"Well, yes, Peter," Eileen joined in, "that's true, but you must realize that you have been living this way for years. You have been trained to know these things, and it is just like second nature to you. You can't expect visitors walking into the community to understand it straight away. It takes time."

Peter gives a subtle shrug like he's just been scolded by Mama. He drinks a large gulp of his brew and flashes a satisfied grin over to me.

One thing is obvious. Peter is having a lot of fun. He runs about the community catalyzing its activities, pouring an inexhaustible stream of energy into the whole, living every moment with every ounce of his being. I had come expecting to meet a Scottish Luther Burbank with straw in his boots, compost in his cuffs, and daisies in his hair, someone who tapped the secrets of nature and who was now so far gone that communication would be difficult at best. Instead, Peter sits at the helm of a community with the aura of a corporate president, the very picture of mental clarity and verbal acuity, with an openness and frankness that blows at your mind like a trombone. He will discuss his successes with no false "gee whiz" humility, and in the same breath, with identical enthusiasm, he will discuss his most intimate and humiliating failures. It is all the same to him. It is the Path.

Peter has been walking that Path for years, and he knows it so well that he has thrown all the maps away. Everything he contacts is a part of the Path.

"Mistakes? I've made so many I can't count them. And everyone was divinely guided, a message to me, something for me to learn. I used to run this community with an iron fist. I didn't consult anyone. When I was moved to act, I acted. When the inspiration came, I didn't wait to see if some committee would approve it. Usually I would get confirmation through Eileen's guidance, but that was all. But last year, I was laid up for a month in the hospital with a gallstone operation. Why? To learn that I couldn't go on this way, and that the community had to learn to run itself without me. We are moving into the age of group consciousness, and I had to learn to work with a group, not as an individual."

Peter holds nothing back. He sits in front of you like an open book. Whatever you want to know, just ask. He will look you straight in the eye and answer.

"Visions? I have never had visions. I don't get guidance,

I don't see things, and I don't hear voices. Nothing! In 1957 I had reached the culmination of this training, a spiritual training you would call it, after which I was supposed to hear voices, get inner guidance, similar to what Eileen receives. It was a small and select group, hand chosen, and everyone had successfully completed the training except me. It was my turn at last. On an appointed day, I was to sit quietly and I would supposedly hear that 'still, small voice within.' I waited. I waited that whole day. Another day, and I sat another eight hours. I just did not hear a thing! My teacher would come up to me in the middle of the day and say: 'Do you hear anything now? Do you hear it now?' I just sat there and shook my head. I had to keep sitting. I really cannot abide sitting, but I did it anyway. Day after day, week after week, I sat. They finally gave up, you see. Nothing! I did not hear a word!

"What I have is intuition. I will just feel like doing something and act in the moment. I never question my intuition. It's always right, even if it seems crazy to me at the time. It is only after looking back that I can see the patterns unfolding in my life. Look at Findhorn! We came to this rubbish dump surrounded by tatty caravans in the middle of winter. Sheer madness! It was only later that the deeper, underlying meaning was revealed. We didn't know anything at that time. If we did, we probably would have fainted from shock at the work that was to be done. The good Lord lets you know a little bit at a time, otherwise your nervous system couldn't take it. Eileen received guidance that thousands of people would be drawn to this, 'My Center of Light.' Well, what could that possibly mean? we thought. Thousands coming to a rubbish dump on the North Sea? Fancy that. But now they come."

Indeed, like moths to light, they come to Findhorn from all over the world. It is a pilgrimage. For what? Most do not know. They are "drawn here," they know not why. They come to learn lessons and to figure out why later. They come not to do obeisance to a Master or to get a peanut dropped into their palm from a shrouded near-saint, nor do they come to mortify the flesh for the spirit in harsh meditative practices or restricted diets. They just come! And as each comes, it is Peter's job to figure out what that person has brought to give. He sees each person as one who has come to give something to the whole, only they usually don't know it themselves. It's Peter's role to help them figure it out.

Skeptics and nonbelievers who come grumbling through the gates are drawn into the community before they know what has hit them. If they have any criticism after that, fine! But now they are part of the whole, the greater family, and it is easier to criticize someone else's family than your "own." Just as there are no "ifs" here, there is no "criticism" either. You "share" with a person—you do not criticize him. It is criticism with compassion. There are no overt attacks, no Synanon let-it-all-hang-out, blood-smoke-passion-caffein-and-neuroses "I hate you, you yellow bastard, for sneaking into my room and ripping off my Ayn Rand book, you little creep!" No, no, no. Try: "Ever since you manifested the only copy of *Revelation* from my room without mentioning it to me, I have felt . . . this . . . something between us, and I'd just like to share it with you." It warms your cockles, and keeps them coming back for more.

And they keep coming, more every year.

Who is this man who seems to be the center of all of this? What is he really doing? He seems so ordinary in most ways. He is the most unlikely person to be the "custodian" of a New Age community. There is nothing gurulike or holy about Peter Caddy. He is not the soft-spoken master gathering the children to his feet. Reality often flies in the face of appearances. He is outwardly middle class, almost priggishly English, niggly about petty details of decorum and form, very much the ex-squadron leader barking out commands. But one sees that inwardly he is a man who is extremely sensitive and intensely motivated. Sufis caution the seeker to look not for the obvious when seeking a teacher. There are countless stories of how ragged and verminous beggars wandering out of the deserts were nothing but saints and sages. This is the twentieth century. How about a clean-cut, fiftyish, former RAF officer with three children and a lovely silver-permed wife living in a trailer park with a garden of delphiniums and marigolds?

Impeccable in speech and manner, Peter speaks in the clipped accentless style of the military. When he speaks, he makes himself very clear. He has a large store of aphorisms and clichés which everyone here knows by heart. He constantly reemphasizes these to all around him. The main principle is that you are what you think, you become what you think, and what you think becomes reality. Therefore, the stress here is on creative and positive thinking. Peter is the embodiment of this. He emanates an overpowering confidence and self-assurance, but he is not arrogant. Despite his dogmatic and blunt approach to life, one does not sense the slightest bit of selfishness. Sometimes there is even a trace of diffidence belying it all. Peter feels that this lifetime and past lifetimes were all training for what is happening right now at Findhorn. And behind it all is the Training, and it is the *one* area about which Peter does not talk very much. All questions are neatly fielded and grounded. There are stories of Tibetan rings, Initiations on Ben Macdhui, Aureolis, Dr. Sullivan, Comte de Saint-Germain, Shambala, Master Rakoczi, and the Rosicrucians. The incongruity of the man screams out at you. The middle-class illusion can be shattered by a torrent of occult and esoteric terms that Peter has mastered and incorporated into what appears to be a carefully designed plan of life. But one gets a very distinct feeling that it is not Peter's plan—it is somebody else's, which raises the further questions of Who and What is the Plan? Peter sometimes seems more of an agent than a Master.

Despite the outrageousness of what he says, you've got to believe him. This man cannot lie. Honesty is the keystone. Everything rests on it. His truthfulness is written across his face in a childlike scrawl. If he tells you his cabbages grew as big as beachballs, you know it is true. When he tells you he is overlighted by the Master of the Seventh Ray, you believe it, even though you don't have a clue as to what the Seventh Ray is. And when he tells you he has been given the Training for lifetimes in order that the Will of God be brought down to earth to fuse with mankind in a new evolutionary leap beginning right here at Findhorn, you say, "Why not?" Whatever the preconceptions that were carried up the tarmac road to Findhorn they have now been blown away like a dandelion thistle in a gale. You are left with a gaping and naked mind in front of one of the most unusual men you are ever likely to meet, sitting quietly in his cedarwood bungalow against a background of the most radiant collection of flowers and plants you have ever seen.

And how do we explain this, Mr. Scholar?

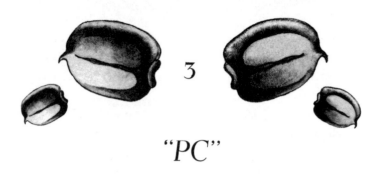

3

"PC"

WE HAVE BEEN SENT BY THE HIGHER ONES TO REVEAL THE
PLAN AND THE WAY. EVERYTHING WITHIN YOUR PLANE OF
EXISTENCE IS KNOWN TO US.

Peter felt shivers going up and down his spine. Each
syllable hung in the air for a full second before slowly drifting into silence—flaccid membranous bubbles that floated
over the room and then burst over the group with a cloying
spray of meaning.

MY CHILDREN . . . FROM HIGHER SPHERES WE DESCEND . . .
TO YOUR EARTHLY PLANE . . . WITH IN-SPI-RA-TION AND IL-LU-
MI-NA-TION!

What was this Power? What was this stuff that filled the
room like hot broth? The throaty voice came from Lucille
Rutterby, a friend of the family who bellowed out the
Sunday hymns with Peter's father from the apse of the
Ruislip Methodist Church in Middlesex. It was a ten-year-
old's bedtime, but tonight Peter sat up and witnessed Mrs.
Rutterby transmitting to the "spiritual circle" his father
Frederick had joined.

THE GREAT SPIRIT IS WITHIN YOU. KNOW THIS, AND YOUR
WALK ALONG THE PATH OF PHYSICAL MATTER CAN BE DONE
WITH EASE AND CERTAINTY.

That walk through physical matter was what brought

Frederick Caddy to Lucille Rutterby's Friday night sessions, for he was crippled by the pain of rheumatoid arthritis. For Frederick Caddy, an ardent practitioner of diet reform and hygienic living, the disease was an anathema and psychic thorn. Determined to rid himself of it in any way possible, he went to every type of doctor and healer in the south of England: osteopaths, chiropractors, naturopaths, iridologists, herbalists, homeopaths. The cure became a desperate mission, a zealous pursuit to extremes that occasioned two sixty-day fasts and numerous visits to camphorous parlors, where Peter would stand and watch in mute and wide-eyed wonder the parched and desiccated old men ceremoniously dispensing unctions or balms whose only noticeable effect was a reeking and howling bad smell.

Disappointed by successive and increasingly spectacular failures, Frederick moved to the mysterious medicine of Lucille Rutterby, a "spiritual healer" gifted with the ability to contact those on the "other side" and seek their help. Her husband, Plato Rutterby, joined her and the Caddys in a circle of friends, meeting once a week to channel and transmit the messages of the great Silver Deer, a former North American Indian chief who soared weekdays among the Celestial Ones and descended on Friday nights to the Earth Plane into this jaunty woman in her thirties who resembled a fresh boiled dumpling in woollies.

When the transmitting began, the dumpling sat bolt upright, squat arms folded across a heaving chest, a stern and imposing countenance crossing the soft moist features, and the words rumbled out, carefully orchestrated and P-R-R-RO-NOUNCED. The usually twitty voice dropped an octave, and it became inflected with the slow, sonorous pulsations of a powerful man.

YOU HAVE NOW STEPPED ACROSS THE BORDER!

From the end of the room a lulling dirge drifted out of the gramophone, a long-playing record full of violins, basso profundo, harps, and scratches. The mongrel dog that had been sleeping at Peter's feet sat up tense and still, its attention riveted on the source of the voice, head cocked like the Victrola logo, eyes fixed upon something above Lucille Rutterby's head. Was he seeing the chief's bonnet?

DO YOU HAVE ANY QUESTIONS? boomed Silver Deer Rutterby from the Land of Light.

"How do I win my school boxing match tomorrow?" ventured Peter.

Laughter rippled through the room.

LOOK HIM IN THE EYE, rumbled out the reply, AND YOU WILL KNOW WHEN HE IS ABOUT TO HIT YOU!

Peter remained silent for the rest of the evening. The others may have laughed, but he didn't. He knew he had been given the right advice, the key to tomorrow's matches. With the Silver Deer's words still echoing in his mind, Peter marched off to school the next morning and knocked his opponent's nose off, winning the school cup. After other sessions and other successes, Peter was convinced that there were beings beyond the physical world, spirits alive and real who could help him if only he would ask. The ten-year-old boy, accepting the reality of Silver Deer without a doubt, stepped across the "border" and experienced the birth of a preadolescent occultism that was of the most pragmatic and down-to-earth nature.

Frederick Caddy, on the other hand, noticing no change in his condition after many sessions with Silver Deer, went back to the family doctor, who diagnosed his condition as kidney stones. When they were removed, the pain subsided, never to return again.

Foolishness? A silly mistake?

No! This was Divine Economy!

To hear Peter explain it, good came out of the pain and suffering that his father experienced because it brought Peter into contact with his first "medium."

Divine Economy! There are no mistakes in Peter's life.

44

Only Divine Economy. Mistakes are mistakes only until their divine meaning is ferreted out. Life's dirty nappies come out of the Caddy wash bleached, folded, and spotless. Calamities are Godsends, personal disasters mere stepping stones on the narrow initiatory path that all tread, but few recognize. Realizing this fact gives Peter the energy and purposeful zeal to bound ahead while the rest of humanity seems to be shuffling along and stepping on each other's heels. Many see Peter as narrow and mistake him for his contrail, but it is his speed which causes the social vapor trails, speed of thought, action, resolve, mind, and intuition. He even errs quickly, but then, are there any mistakes?

Divine Economy is Jungian Synchronicity mixed with a Buckie Fullerism: "God does more with less—simultaneously." There are *no* random actions or occurrences. Life is stuffed with meaning, bursting like a potato sack. The slightest alteration and expansion of perception pulls the cotton strings on the burlap sack and the potatoes pour out about your feet like anxious gremlins. Every potato can be boiled and buttered—all depends on your appetite. And PC has an enormous appetite. No potato left unturned; every sack of happenstance is vigorously shaken until every little loose implication falls out. Peter is full of stories confirming and illustrating Divine Economy, incidents demonstrating a pact with fate so firm and fierce that every waking moment of his life seems magical and blessed, everything working out exactly and precisely according to the Plan. Peter positively revels in it, glories in it, loves it, constantly expresses sheer amazement and gratitude for the absolute efficiency of it. CAN'T YOU SEE IT??? PC wants to know. Great waves of belly laughter roar out at what someone else might call a chance coincidence. Not for PC. It is not small at all. It was God's next move in a game where there are no competitors. Cosmic giveaway checkers. Who can get rid of everything first? Peter pours out his heart and soul to life, giving whatever he has, and God just delights in it, giving it right back to Peter threefold.

Your move, Peter!

Lucille Rutterby may have been your normal "medium," but Peter was never to be a normal "seeker." He grew up oxen strong, stubbornly resisting his father's iron-willed Ten Commandment orthodoxy. Despite Frederick Caddy's forays into the spiritual world, he remained a staunch Methodist, rigid and dogmatic about God. Church was twice on Sunday with a few visits sprinkled throughout the week for good measure. But Peter had other ideas.

At seventeen, Peter was taken to meet the managing director of J. Lyons & Co. Ltd., the world's largest caterers, whereupon it was arranged that he would take a five-year director's apprenticeship starting at the Regent Palace Hotel with a year in the kitchens, working through every branch of the operation, from waiting to cakemaking, from the Cadby Hall factories to the Coventry Street Corner House.

During his first year in the kitchens, a "chance" meeting with his future brother-in-law brought him into contact with a fellowship of the original Christian Rosenkreutz Rosicrucians, not the AMORCS from San Jose who often advertise in magazines, but the older European branch, undiluted, original vintage. He was accepted as a member, and if his contacts with Silver Deer planted the seeds of pragmatic occultism, then his studies in the Crotona Fellowship under the tutelage of one Dr. Sullivan positively cultured it. During the day Peter was the white-smocked caterer, broiling fish and roasting tatties, while at night he entered into a world of ancient mysteries, a time warp into the Brotherhood, the Fraternitas Rosae Crucis. It was a world of the precise understanding of the law of cause and effect, where Will merges with Imagination to form the Idea which in the Mind becomes Desire and finally Physical Reality. The Seven Worlds: God, Virgin Spirits, Divine Spirits, Life Spirits, Thought, Desire, and the Physical—the Septenary Principle of evolution and creation. Bound by strict rules and separated from the exoteric world, it was a brotherhood members could easily recognize, impossible to crack unless welcomed, obscure and secretive, the essence of an ancient wisdom that traces its origins to Egypt. Rosicrucian symbology is contained in the writings of Shakespeare, Goethe, and Bacon, which the initiate can see, reading between and through the lines to discover hidden truths. To this day, Peter will say little about it.

The war began, and the twenty-two-year-old PC went with his new Training and one last piece of advice from Dr. Sullivan: "All will be well, but volunteer for nothing." And he didn't. PC's war was not spent in trenches, bombers, or fatigues, but in officers' messes, dances, tennis shorts, conferences, and airplanes shuttling from one place to another. As a commissioned catering officer, he never saw a dead body or heard a gunshot. If there was a war going on, Peter's measure of it was in oranges and apples and in lecturing airmen about the necessity and rectitude of eating synthetic soya sausages, which Peter abhorred and rarely ate.

The youngest squadron leader in the catering branch of the Royal Air Force, Peter had privileges befitting the command caterer to the largest front of the war, the Burma campaign. Known by some as the "playboy of the East," uprightly muscular, with a golden tennis-in-the-afternoon complexion, a cantilevered jaw, and bright squirrel eyes, he charmed his way right up the pecking order as well as the necking one. War was for those who wanted it, fighting was for fighters, but for Peter it was a carte blanche ticket to half the world on any military transport—to dances, tennis, swimming, mountaineering, pony trekking, and chances that no boy from Ruislip could turn down. The good life eventually came to an inglorious and painful end —but that was later. For the duration of the war Peter was waltzing at top speed through all the social amenities great Mother England could lavish on her faithful.

Peter took advantage of all opportunities. An officer in wartime had sweeping powers, could make snap decisions, initial requisitions and dockets in the blink of an eye. In other words, PC could let out his wings and fly! And fly he did. He was the arcane Milo Minderbinder of the East, seizing every opportunity to delve into places ancient and esoteric in order to further the Training.

At the Cawnpore Airbase in India, Peter formed a Mountaineering Club and took Rover-Scout crews on various treks into the Himalayas. Having read the climbing books by Spencer Chapman, Peter was particularly interested and intrigued by the Valley of the Flowers and the mysterious man who was said to dwell near there, the Master of Badrinath.

The trail to the Valley of the Flowers runs sharply up and down, descending deeply into ravines and canyons. You can see the tops of the mountains which are your goal, but before you get there you must cross row after row of smaller mountain ridges. Finally, at the last pass a brilliant white panorama opens up and the vast sweep of the Himalayas is before you like snow diamond crystal cut into a cobalt sky. Below is the valley, a bright carpet of a thousand million flowers: forget-me-nots, blue poppies, and purple asters; yellow, gold, and purple primulas; anemones clinging to rocky slopes; wild irises bursting forth from bogs; golden calendulas bunched along the banks of streams. Following ritual paths, Peter spent days visiting "holy stations." Each day he looked for a sign of the Master of Badrinath. He asked his servant to go ahead of him and inquire, but nothing could be discovered.

On the last day of the two-week trek, Peter's party of eight arrived at their dak bungalow tired and weary. Peter had by that time given up hope of meeting this man whom Spencer Chapman had encountered at 18,000 feet wearing nothing but a loincloth, a man who spoke perfect English and who was conversant with the latest world events, which he said he just "picked" out of the air.

Most of the party had begun to fall asleep when the normally grumbly group captain, a hot-headed man cast in the original imperial mold who saw "wogs" instead of Indians, strode into the bungalow, raving to the tired troops about a wonderful Indian he had met at the bazaar. Peter was astonished at the sudden change in the group captain's attitude and wondered who this Indian might be.

Two elegantly dressed servants appeared and immediately began heating water. By this time, the dozing and napping airmen were awake, eying with intense interest the boxes of Brooke Bond Tea and Peak Frean Biscuits. Where had these Indians obtained stores that not even the command catering officer could get? As they watched and waited, a group of holy men gathered around their bungalow and sat, still and quiet. And then in flowed a very old man with long white hair and beard. Along with a great broad smile, he brought a great rush of vital energy into the room and a second retinue of servants. It was an atmosphere of happiness so palpable you could almost wrap it up and keep it.

The white-haired man was seated and asked the Englishmen to join him in tea. Soon all were happily drinking and conversing with this saintly man. An officer brought out a camera, whereupon the man politely held up his hand and refused. It was then that Peter was sure who his guest was —Ram Sareek Singh, the Master of Badrinath. Peter remembered the stories; those who had tried to take his picture always experienced blank film or vanishing cameras. No one had ever been able to take his photograph, not even his friend Chapman, who tried several times. "You see, my friends, there are those who would take my picture and worship *it*, instead of God. So there should be no pictures."

For Peter it was one of the most inspiring moments in his life, to be in the presence of this vital being. Here, at last, was a true Holy Man, not one moping about in sackcloth and ashes, begging on his haunches in a pile of filth. Ram Sareek Singh was a zestful man, over ninety years old, who enjoyed life and spread that joy wherever he went. This was a breath of fresh air in the rank stuffiness of Indian spirituality, a being as radiant and alive as the flower-strewn valley. The sunlit peaks of the Himalayan dawn were shining through this grinning, golden man who bubbled with laughter.

Ram Sareek Singh confirmed something that Peter had felt throughout his spiritual training: that if something was "right," it had to be right on all levels. It was no use talking about "love" unless it was reflected in every waking moment of your life. It was no use talking about "spirituality" unless you could demonstrate it. It was no use having your head in the clouds unless you could bring heaven down to earth in your daily life. After Peter had been told by his brother-in-law that it took lifetimes of evolution to become a "realized" man, he asked if it could be done in one lifetime. When he was told that it was impossibly difficult, Peter turned to him and said, "I am *going* to do it in one!" For him it was all or nothing. Ram Sareek Singh has been his inspiration ever since their one meeting.

Peter naïvely dedicated himself to becoming a "realized" man, a man totally and completely dedicated to being God's Plan on Earth. Because he knew that he was to be a channel for God's will, he had to perfect himself in body and mind. His training with Dr. Sullivan, particularly in the areas of positive thinking through the teachings of Aureolis, became his beacon of strength in the Royal Air Force. Having developed a strong will in overcoming his father's stubborn ways, he trained it further through various physical disciplines and the Rosicrucian teachings and then forged it in the overwhelming logistics of feeding a million men during a war in countries where food was chronically short. By running miles every day in the hot sun, swimming whenever he could, and undertaking arduous climbs in the Himalayas, his body became a powerful instrument of his will. As the ultimate test of both will and body, Peter organized an expedition to Tibet right at the end of the war.

More than a country or a culture, Tibet was for Peter the ancient capital of a world spiritual civilization. Again and again, he was refused permission by his superior officer, but because of the Training, Peter could not accept no for an answer. Everything he learned from Dr. Sullivan and Aureolis was brought into action. Persistently and doggedly he kept at his base commander until he finally relented.

Sixteen experienced men were chosen, including a chaplain and a doctor. No one from the West had entered through the Jelep La Pass since two officers died there earlier in the war. The goal was Gyantse, a holy city of monasteries some 300 miles into the interior. As time was short, they would have to travel some 30 miles a day on foot at elevations between 15,000 and 18,000 feet, in temperatures down to 40 below zero.

Provisions and equipment were secured, the very best the RAF could offer, right down to tinned peaches and cream. Planes were obtained to ferry both men and stores to Calcutta. From there they were to convoy to the train station, where they would catch a train to Kalimpong, their starting point. At the airport the men and provisions were placed in two trucks and headed for the city. But Calcutta! It was no longer a city. It was a diseased animal, mad and furious with pain and hunger. Food was unobtainable, prices were soaring, money was worthless, and people were panicking. Peter had heard there might be riots, but this! It was insanity!

Around the convoy swarmed gleaming bright eyes that

clung and pierced like hungry ticks. The men and food were surrounded by a sea of anger and yellow-stained eyeballs where white teeth flashed unintelligible curses in the sun. The two transport trucks wended their way painfully through the streets, encircled by a special detachment of warrant officers, every man on and off the truck nervously fingering cocked carbines. Stones rattled the cab tops, a knife tore the canvas, the vehicles swayed against the press of the swelling crowds. Every yard brought another hungry soul, eying the provisions with a lust no man should see. *In solitary, stony fastness among the mountains there is a strange market where you can barter the vortex of life for boundless bliss.* A case of peaches fell off the truck, and three hundred people fought and scrabbled for it. The two trucks sped off in the temporary release of the mob. They arrived at the railway station, where they boarded the jammed train for Kalimpong and headed toward the solitary and stony fastness of Tibet.

Countless obstacles had been overcome. Peter's faith in the Training, the techniques taught to him by Aureolis, knew no bounds. It was a powerful magic that continuously grew through the war years. It was luxurious and thick, wrapped about him like an invisible vine, protecting him while reaching out with tendrils to enwrap all that he touched, transforming people and opening up paths.

Yet the Training was not something of the past, it was happening right now, this was *all* a part of the Training. It was all preparation. For what? What was he being trained for? To what end was his body and spirit being forged and shaped? The forces that moved through his life had become increasingly powerful. His mind was giving way to a surging intuitive grasp and knowledge that existed only in the moment. While plans became less and less meaningful, the meaning of his life seemed more and more "planned." Everything was leading to some *thing*, that he could feel, but there was nothing that he could see as yet that would tell him what it was to be. There was a purpose, of that there could be no doubt. It would be revealed to him in its own time.

From Kalimpong to the top of the Jelep La Pass the Sikkim Stairs rise 10,000 feet in nine miles to an elevation of 14,390 feet. Peter and fifteen other officers and airmen began the trek in two parties, Peter's party in advance and the other a day behind. The nine-foot-wide track up the "Stairs" was partially paved with cobblestones in order to withstand the torrential rains and the endless succession of caravans and pack animals.

Peter stood at the edge of the dense rain forest. He looked down and saw everywhere tiny sluglike leeches moving toward one point: his feet. Pencil thin, brown, and slimy, they moved with one mind toward his pink skin. Behind him he could hear the muleteers laughing at their jokes. Their legs, like Peter's, were bare, but the other men were dressed to the neck with double socks, gaiters, breeches, and buttoned collars and sleeves. They sweated like pigs in the boiling dankness, but their fear of leeches was greater than their discomfort.

Eighty cases had been packed on twenty-eight mules. They were gaily decorated animals with ribbons and tassles about their manes and tails, and strings of neck bells rang softly as they patiently awaited the continuation of their journey. Two of the muleteers were adjusting their loads, softly padding about in their thick carpet slippers to each of their lot, jabbering to the mules and each other, tightening cinches, laughing at a joke that never seemed to end. Every time they laughed, their white teeth would ignite and they would steal a look at the overdressed English as if the joke was on them.

Peter glanced ahead to Kanchenjunga, blocking out the native cackle, and in the swirling gray mists that surrounded the lofty peak, he lost himself in thought. . . .

THOSE WHOSE HOUR HAD COME . . . DARK GREW THE SPACE
BETWEEN THE SPHERES . . . THE HOUR OF SACRIFICE HAD
ARRIVED . . . THE TIMELESS ONES ENTERED INTO TIME . . . AND
LO, THE WORK PROCEEDS. . . .

*Can it be described, that perfect knowing? When every
cell knows more than the mind can know, knowing the
perfection, the real presence and absolute rightness of one
moment? We are cast into infinite levels of knowing. I
know that time is like an invisible point in space through
which my conscious mind can burst like a lightning flash,
a split-second expansion and disappearance in the Real
Life; the knowing that this is how it has been designed,
planned, executed, lived, and now relived, and that I am
in that point of space and time as testimony to a perfectly
executed destiny. Destiny! It is so thick, I could brush it
away like a cobweb. I know this is the Way, The Way . . .*
a great burst of noisy hooves, dislodged stones, and clang-
ing bells broke his reverie and signaled the caravan's departure.

Peter looked about at his seven companions and then
marched to the head of the column. He set a slow steady
pace. Sudden and frequent clatter marked the mules slipping on the wet cobbles under their heavy loads. Water was
dripping off everything, a steady percolation into one great
organic stew of rotting bark, moldy leaves, thick leathery
vines, and huge trunks of squat and twisted trees enclasped
by ferns, moss, and lichen. Every plant and every tree was
woven into another. To his left, a black and rotten tree lay
collapsed and dead, rows of crusty orange fungi clinging to
its flank, descending into the humus.

Everything was eating, gnawing, and regurgitating.
Plants were eating insects, insects eating animals, animals
eating plants, and the earth was eating it all. It seemed a
fitting start to Peter's pilgrimage. He was going to a land
thought to be holy of Holies, most sacred of all, the spiritual center of the great world Brotherhood, Shambala!

This was the very axis of the Earthly Wheel of Life, turning through the Litany of Death, the World of Illusion, the Four Kingdoms, the Regions of Coarse Desires, and the World of Maya; the greed, lust, and glut of the senses in the relative world were as teeming and destructive to the spirit as was to the body this rotting forest jungle through which the Sikkim Stairs passed to the heavens, the rooftops of the world.

Up the Sikkim Stairs, skinny dogs, peaches, and officers. Click, click, click of the mules' hooves through the rain forest. They ascended to alpine meadows, to conifers and familiarity. Through Jelep La it grew cold, crisp, and dry. Snow fell as they marched higher to Sebu La and 17,000 feet. Here the air was thin and bone dry. Water poured out with every breath. And something permeated the air which was not oxygen, not nitrogen, not ozone, not molecules, but the breath of the gods, rushing out with the great gusts of winds bringing new life and a cutting clarity of mind.

After Sebu La, they were alternately chased by blinding duststorms and late winter blizzards. Supplies were lost as frightened mules bolted, scattering their loads across the plain or down steep ravines. Officers went snowblind, or collapsed from exhaustion. Tempers replaced the romance; Tibet had become bitterly real, survival paramount. After a 30-mile push through heavy snow, the party regrouped to discover a member missing. Against the advice of his exhausted Tibetan guide, Peter plowed back into the teeth of the storm and walked another 30 miles before finding the lost member.

Peter had gained complete mastery over his body. To other members of his party, his strength and endurance appeared supernatural. But Peter knew it was not his body, but a force passing through his mind, the power of his will.

Peter would awaken the party at 3:30 A.M. every morning so that they could set out by 4:00 A.M. They would march steadily for 30 miles and then retire to dak bungalows for the remainder of the day and wait out the fierce windstorms that blew across the plateau in the afternoons. It became a routine: up early in the darkness, moving through the dust and cold, past vagabonds and unseen travelers in the night. At dawn they could see in the distance prayer flags flapping from cairns, tattered and shredded by the ceaseless winds. During the day, they would meet wool-bearing caravans heading for India. Sometimes there were sparse fields of barley, buckwheat, or turnips. Nomads with thick beards and sheepskin coats tied at their waist would grin at them through blackened butter-smeared faces as they passed with wives, yaks, and children.

After seven days they saw Phari on the horizon, appearing in the distance like a medieval castle abandoned on a plain of despair. The clear air made it visible a good 20 miles before arrival, the reflections from the rocky plain magnifying the walled city until it danced and shimmered upon the land. As the hours ticked by, Phari loomed larger and blacker on the horizon. And suddenly you are upon it, looking up its ramparts to an impregnable fortress of frozen stone. They walked through the gates into streets of excrement and gutters of urine. The city, decorated with bones and carcasses, stared at them in fear and insolence. Foul-smelling children tugged at their coats, ulcerous sores across their faces, teeth rotten and brown, their hair matted and tangled like oil-soaked mops. Yellow ice covered the frozen pools of offal. Great black ravens sat calmly rooted to rooftops, idly waiting for the smell of death to rise from the houses below. Intermingled with it all was a gagging smell of rancid yak butter issuing forth from alleys and passages until one suspected every building, stone, person, and animal had been soaked in it.

They couldn't leave fast enough, and kept marching. After ten days, and 300 miles, they saw shining on the horizon the golden roofs of the Rarkor Choide monastery, looking like an Arthur Clarke village of the future on some remote and desolate planet, strangely futuristic in style and shape against the pale ocher hills. Roads converged into one bringing to the holy city, herdsmen, monks, pilgrims, tradesmen, and eight sunburned Englishmen.

In Gyantse they were warmly received by the abbot of the monastery. They rested one day until the second party arrived. That night a great dinner was given in their honor. Clothes and songs were exchanged, and a great abundance of barley beer was consumed. The party settled in for a few days.

The next day, Peter wandered alone about the monastery.

Why had he come to Tibet? Was there something in this monastery that would tell him the answer?

Was there something to be discovered? Could anything be discovered on such a short trip?

He *knew* he was to come to Tibet, and now it was the end of the trip and the question was why? What had been the purpose?

He continued to walk through the spacious rooms and corridors while he thought. The cold thin air blew down the passages and passed through and over him.

Everywhere in Tibet he had seen poverty, disease, unhappiness, and filth. Here it was different. In Gyantse, the people were healthy and rosy-cheeked. There was a joy and song in their voices that he had not encountered anywhere else in Tibet. But Peter knew that Gyantse was not the wellspring of Tibetan consciousness, but one of its last strongholds, a cultural anchor that was rusted solid to its mooring of rocks, mountains, and ritual.

All about him in the monastery were noises like the amplified monitoring of some huge physical body. In distant rooms he could hear strange instruments, rattles, and dull thuds. Great surges of sound issued forth from the fleshy bellies of a thousand monks. The vibrations merged with the fetid and grimy dust, the incense, and dung fire smoke. Butter lamps flickered in his eyes while deep drums signaled far across the hills. Tankas portraying horrifying deities stared from their protected alcoves, violent cosmic swords in hand ready to slit the throat of astral interlopers. Awesome trips to hell flaming in their eyes, the masters of evil lined the galleries to banish the darkness of the subconscious.

Tibet was celebrating the death of the ego, but there was another dimension to the ritual. Tibet was celebrating its own death.

Like a senile organism that has lost its coordination and vitality, Tibet lay helplessly on the roof of the world dying. All the sounds converged into one long mournful moan from the quivering and shrinking innards of a dying beast; its breath was long, hard, and labored.

The monks and genyens were performing the funeral rites with a mechanical precision: the collective death of the psyche, preparing for earth sinking into water, fire into rock, life into death. Tibet was dying. A five-thousand-year-old culture was crumbling under the onslaught of new civilizations. Its carefully constructed dogmas were now confounded by even greater ones, more mysterious ones, and the elaborately crafted rituals and ceremonies of thousands of years were now decrepit and sickly. Relentless forces were moving across the face of the planet. Neither isolation, nor altitude, nor language, nor custom could resist the inevitable changes. Tibet was an old body lying and waiting calmly for death. Soon the Chinese would storm across its borders and strike the death blow.

O Nobly born, forget not these words: Alas, when the Uncertain Experiencing of Reality is dawning upon me here, with every thought of fear and terror or awe for all set aside, May I recognize whatever appears as the reflection of mine own consciousness. . . . May I not fear the bands of Wrathful Deities, mine own thought forms. . . .

A white sun poured into one of the halls, cutting shafts into the smoke and dust.

Peter had come to see a great spiritual culture, a race evolved since the beginnings of history. Tibet was thought at one time to be the highest reflection of a God-state on earth. What Peter found was the last shrinking vestige of a world civilization. This was not the culture that would bring the Kingdom of God to man. It was dying as surely as the rest of the world was dying in air raids and bombs. It was experiencing the collapse of its institutions, the withdrawal of energies, the end of its history. Peter had come to Tibet to know that there was no religion that could bring God to man, that there was no race that would bring about peace on earth, that there was no culture that would be the pattern for a new civilization on earth. Everything must be new. Man must now go to God. The Kingdom was within, and all wisdom and understanding must come from the God within, through each individual, not from the outside. It was a long journey to discover what was within himself all the time. And now that he knew, it was a quick and easy journey back.

Peter's whole life until Tibet had been directed toward the outer: action, movement, authority, will. It had been a star-crossed existence which gave him everything he wanted. Life seemed inordinately easy and simple—magically blessed. He had all the niceties of a successful career, a lovely wife and children, a sports car back home in England, prestige, status, and respect. His trip to Tibet brought to a close his first season as a man.

During those twenty-eight years he had molded and changed the world to suit his will and needs. Standing at the furthermost extension of his career and desires in the Rarkor Choide monastery, he had reached the end of his journey into physical worlds. If everything to this point had been an exploration of the outer worlds, after Tibet Peter was to experience an inner journey to all the heavens and hells that lay within him, until finally he was to be stripped of everything he possessed: his hopes, his position, his home, his family, his ideals, and even his self-respect. He was to be laid bare and exposed to forces that hurtled at him with unnerving power and speed. He was to experience the very depths of despair and hopelessness.

The Training would take strange and bizarre twists and turns with his and others' lives; events that would shatter anybody else's sensibilities would occur with terrifying frequency and regularity. It was no longer to be a "normal" life. Peter had wanted to "do it" in one life, and, having invoked that thought form, would have to pay the consequences. He would be battered and knocked about until finally, without the arrogance and hubris of the brash squadron leader marching up the Sikkim Stairs with destiny in his pocket, he would and could give up his life to serve God in a most unusual way.

Within a few days after being repatriated to England, Peter met Sheena Govan on the weekend train to his home in Christchurch, Hampshire. She became his teacher, lover, and wife, and the next five years were spent learning lesson after lesson through Sheena's loving but insistent probing of Peter's weaknesses.

Peter, the iron-willed and dynamic squadron leader whose being vibrated with energy, ideas, and plans of action, was struck dumb in the presence of this woman. Another part of his being was born, the side of love and compassion. The loneliness of being on top, of being a leader, of being ahead, the loneliness of a life ordered and regulated, crashed into the vastness of feeling and love, a love which shattered the old constructs and wiped out the narrow paths he wandered, a love which scrapped the well-laid plans and beggared all that he had ever felt.

Sheena Govan was a radiantly beautiful woman who had been steeped in religion and Godly pursuits from birth. Her mother and father had founded the worldwide evangelical Faith Mission. Born in the "faith," suckled on service to humanity, and weaned on complete dedication to God's Will, she led a life totally devoted to God.

Peter became not only her husband but one of many disciples who looked to Sheena for spiritual counsel and advice. In the relationship, Peter experienced an extraordinary reversal of roles. Sheena's life was totally occupied with attending to visitors. She was the dominant person in the relationship, and he, recognizing someone far greater than himself, became submissive. The command caterer to the Burma campaign made the tea and arranged the biscuits for those who sought Sheena's teachings. Having been a leader for so many years, he was now cast into the role of server. He cooked the meals, did the washing up, cleaned the flat, and looked after Sheena. He was transformed by her words and grace as he listened to the counsel offered disciples.

Up to this point in his life, Peter had pursued enlightenment and knowledge through the esoteric teachings of the Rosicrucian Order. In contrast to this, Sheena offered him the understanding of the birth of the "Christ within" through a classical initiatory path. He chose the latter, and got rid of every last one of his books on the occult mysteries. For Peter, Sheena was a midwife attending the birth of the Christ consciousness within, and she did it with a perfect balance of love and wisdom.

I have had a long preparation. I have been called upon to give up or had everything taken away on all levels. It starts with giving up one's will. I was taught how to develop my will through the teachings of Dr. Sullivan, and I developed a tremendous will. This was demonstrated in Tibet, when through the power of my will I was able to do fantastic feats of physical endurance. When crossing the Himalayas to Yatung in Tibet, one of our party was lost in a storm, and I had to go back across that 18,000-foot path, a distance of 30 miles, in the snow, in which I wore out a Tibetan who had been born there. This "will" I had to give up to God. Then comes giving up everything on the physical plane—the first initiation. When my first marriage broke up after meeting Sheena, I lost all of my material possessions, and this was to happen again and again, until I no longer depended on them but rather looked to God for my sustenance. Then there was the second initiation, the giving up on the emotional level. This occurred during Sheena's and my relationship when I was asked to give Sheena up, to place my love for God above my love for a woman. The third was giving up everything on the mental level, the concepts, the intellect, and the ideas that one has imposed upon the world, and to release these and see the world again as a child, with fresh eyes and an open mind. And the fourth is the crucifixion, when one is stripped of everything at once—one's hopes, ideals, self-respect . . . everything. All have to go, so one is left with nothing but God and one realizes that of oneself, one is nothing. The personality is crucified, and the darkness descends. And then comes the fifth initiation, the resurrection and ascension, when one realizes My Father and I are one.

Sheena showed me the way, and I began to experience this path. It was as though I thought I was a pool of clear water, but she would come along with a stick and stir that pool, bringing all the mud that was on the bottom to the surface where it could be seen and recognized and removed.

Peter's training under Sheena continued for five long years. During that time, he was posted as commanding officer to the Innsworth School of Cookery, his success there in boosting morale and fostering leadership subsequently earning him a place at the Royal Air Force Staff College. After a year at the college, he was sent to a newly created post in the Middle East. Before he left for his tour of duty, Sheena told him that it had been revealed to her that they were no longer to be man and wife: they would still have a close relationship, but the marriage was over and it was the end of an apprenticeship. Peter was to go on to a new chapter in his life, for his true partner was somewhere in the world waiting to join him. And so the husband-wife relationship between Peter and Sheena came to a close, as dramatically and suddenly as they had come together, but the teacher-pupil relationship remained. Peter left for the Middle East somewhat shattered, but also expectant of what was to come.

While in Iraq, at the large Habbaniya airbase, he was invited by a wing commander to dine at his home with his wife and children. Andrew Combe had read Peter's article on leadership in the *RAF Quarterly* and wanted to meet the author. Peter's "patterned life" followed form, for that evening he felt a link with the only woman in the room, Andrew's wife Eileen. He did not feel love, emotion, or deep feelings, simply an intuitive prompting that suggested that he and Eileen were close in some way. He put it out of his mind, however, and the weeks and months passed.

Peter and Eileen would encounter each other occasionally, sometimes around the airbase. As Peter moved about the world on his duties, the infrequent meetings occurred just often enough to keep a formal relationship alive.

During a visit to Jerusalem, Peter was sitting on a hill overlooking the city and seemed to hear a voice which said Eileen was his other half. He immediately rejected the idea: Eileen was married, she had five children, and there was no love between them. But because of what Sheena had said, he was not entirely unreceptive to the idea and silently asked that if this was to be so, that proof be given.

Peter knew all was not well between Andrew and Eileen. Andrew's work in Moral Rearmament was a major source of conflict; he was seldom home with her or the children but rather going about on lectures promoting the Four Standards: Absolute Unselfishness, Absolute Purity, Absolute Love, and Absolute Honesty. During one of his visits to Habbaniya, a mutual friend took Andrew aside and told him that if he did not take some of that Absolute Love and Unselfishness home, he was in danger of losing his wife. Andrew reportedly responded by saying that Moral Rearmament was more important. When Peter heard this, it seemed to confirm his inner voice.

Peter immediately sought out Eileen and found her alone at home. The incident with the voice in Jerusalem was recounted to her, she sitting at one end of a long couch, and he at the other. She did not know what to think at this rather bold and pointed announcement. She agreed with Peter on one point: that if they were to be brought together, it would be God's doing, certainly not hers. To Eileen, Peter seemed to be a very serious young man. He constantly talked about things she had never heard of, "gibberish" about the occult, the Brotherhood, and the Hierarchy, soul halves and mates, all of which made no sense to her. She had found most of Andrew's friends from Moral Rearmament to be a rather pompous and self-righteous lot, and Peter seemed to follow suit.

Peter continued to fly about the world on one mission after another, occasionally stopping in Habbaniya, but never for long. A year after he and Eileen had met, both were scheduled to return to London. Peter was called back for a conference, and Andrew decided to send Eileen home six weeks before the end of his tour of duty. Peter arranged to meet Eileen's plane in Tripoli and joined her and the children on the flight to London. Eileen went to her country home, and Peter went to stay with friends. Later that week, Sheena was to join them both at dinner and the theater to celebrate Eileen's birthday, but because she was stricken with a migraine headache that afternoon, Peter and Eileen went without her. After a pleasant evening, Peter took her home.

There, whatever barrier or constraint that had been between them vanished. The years of mechanically fulfilling the function of wife and childbearer had gnawed away at Eileen's feelings and emotions until she had become a granite stoic about marriage and love. She had never thought of leaving Andrew, for in most respects he had been a good husband. But once away from him, the military, and the past, she felt all the frustration and tension of those cold empty years dissolve in the warmth of love and tears.

Eileen wrote to Andrew the next morning, and the gates of hell crashed open. Andrew came immediately to London and took the children away while Peter and Eileen were out. Possession being nine-tenths of the law, Eileen knew it was over. The children were lost. No court in the land would give them back. She was the transgressor, the sinner, the curse on family and home. Andrew locked the children in his family home and forbade Eileen to come near. Gifts were sent back unopened, letters still sealed. No phone calls were allowed. The joy of new love was tempered by the emptiness of her loss.

Peter and Eileen decided to get out of London for a few days, to think things over and look at the future. They drove to Glastonbury and stopped at a sanctuary for a few moments of silence. Eileen sat still, trying to quiet the mind that cried for the children.

Everything grew still.

There was not a sound to be heard. No birds, no cars, no children, no breathing, nothing. Stillness, richer than gold and vast as space, replaced the cries. The mind stumbled into a new dimension.

Slowly and deliberately, a clear voice emerged from the silence: "Be still . . . and know that I am God."

Stillness. Silence.

Nobody had spoken.

"You have taken a very big step in your life. Listen to Me, and all will be well."

Eileen opened her eyes and looked about her. There was nobody except Peter. She closed her eyes again.

"Let not your heart be troubled. Know who I am. I am closer to you than your breath, than your hands and feet. Trust in Me."

And so Eileen sat and listened, opening a chapter of her life that would lead her and Peter on an incredible journey, not through space, but into consciousness and action. Eileen the spinner, Peter the weaver.

Every day, she received messages in that same clear voice. The daily messages guided them step by step through the complex and intricate circumstances in which they found themselves. Nevertheless, Eileen had difficulty in accepting what was happening. Peter, on the other hand, had absolute faith in them as God's guidance. Despite her lingering doubts, she wrote everything down, and Peter obeyed the instructions to the letter.

Eileen became pregnant, and later that year, Peter was sent back to the Middle East. Sheena had become very ill and contacted Peter for help. Eileen cared for her while he was away, for she had received in guidance that she was to look upon Peter's ex-wife as her teacher and a source of wisdom.

But her relationship with Sheena was strained and uncomfortable. The fact that Peter still regarded her as his spiritual authority made Eileen feel insecure and secondary. Officially they were still married, and Eileen, cut off from her family, felt her existence had become fragile and precarious. The sorrow of losing the children remained. It was with her constantly in everything she did. At times she could understand it, but in the next moment it all seemed wrong.

After the birth of their first child, Peter resigned his commission in the RAF, feeling the lessons to be learned there were completed. In a conversation with Peter shortly after, Sheena instructed him to separate from Eileen for a while because they were placing the relationship above God and that time apart would help them grow. Peter was to go away, and Eileen was to live with Sheena's disciple, Dorothy Maclean.

Peter went to Ireland, where after a stint as a farmhand he found a job as a salad boy in a small country inn. The woman who hired him had no idea that Peter had at one time been responsible for feeding a million men, and he didn't tell her. She would have her salads "just so" and was constantly complaining and criticizing her ex-command caterer. As much as Peter detested his job and being away from Eileen, he accepted Sheena's pronouncement in faith and worked without protest.

But Eileen did not have the strength to endure another "splitting up," nor did she have the same faith in Sheena's judgments as did Peter. The separation was intolerable, and the accumulated sadness and pain of losing the children redoubled her sorrow. She did not know where Peter was or how to contact him.

Sheena was aware of her suffering, but criticized her, feeling this weakness indicated lack of spiritual strength. The migraines that affected Sheena increased in frequency and made her sharp and irritable. Whatever truth her criticism contained, it also carried the extra weight of the pain and suffering that she was experiencing. Eileen would sit up half the night, soothing her, praying and meditating for her, but when morning came, more abuse and criticism would pour forth.

Eileen was reaching breaking point. Walking home from the flat to Dorothy's she felt her mind starting to slip. In the dampness and fog, she began falling apart. Everything started to turn black, and when she reached home, hungry for sympathy from Dorothy, she found the house empty. The gas stove was turned on, and Eileen laid her head inside the open oven door to go to sleep.

At that moment her brother walked into the flat, saw her, and slapped her across the face.

He took her to a farm, where she was joined by her five

children. She was shocked and dazed. The mute and bitter woman gave up everything: Peter, the guidance, God, Sheena, everything. It was over. It was through, finished, a bad dream.

Eileen was beyond any and all feelings.

When Peter heard the news of Eileen, he collapsed. He knew that each step of his life, every incident, was of divine importance. Others would see him as hopelessly mad or egomaniacal because they could not know how sure this man was of his destiny. But something about this latest episode shook him to his roots. Something was wrong with the Plan. He walked away from his job and just wandered about. Nothing seemed "guided" or "divinely economical" anymore. Somehow, he had failed or had been failed. The powerful body that vaulted over the Himalayas began wasting away. In a month, he lost thirty pounds and his hair began to turn white. He was emaciated and weak.

There was a time in Ireland when I couldn't see. I was in the dark. I couldn't see what it was all about, and I had a glimpse that this was to be my crucifixion. You see, Eileen and I knew we were cornerstones of God's plan for the New Age. We had been brought together for that purpose. We were to be one of the foundations upon which the New Age was to be built. We could only do this work together. I knew God's plan. But this I didn't understand. Without her, I would be useless. I'm only one half. I wouldn't be able to fulfill God's plan. This plan was dependent upon our union, and she had failed. I couldn't sleep at night. I didn't want anything to eat. I couldn't see anybody. All that I was aware of was this overriding sense and weight of failure. My health had gone, job had gone, hopes gone, ideals gone, plans gone. I didn't have a single possession. I had nowhere to go. The child was gone. Nothing.

Peter finally ended up in the New Forest, where his son was being cared for by Sheena. The shock of seeing this tiny hapless body crying without his mother was the last shock Peter could take. Like an automaton, he borrowed a car and drove straight through the night to the farm Eileen had been taken to. He arrived early in the morning and crawled into a ditch outside the farmhouse.

He waited. Cold water soaked his shoes and cuffs.

Dawn came, and he waited.

The house came to life, but Peter remained motionless. Through the kitchen window he could see Eileen and Andrew. They were talking over breakfast. Peter remained crouched and still. He knew exactly what he was to do. The minutes turned into hours, and still he waited. Eight o'clock, nine o'clock, nine thirty, nine forty-five. Peter waited.

At ten o'clock Andrew came out the front door and started his car. Peter watched intently. Andrew went back into the house once more and then came out and drove away.

Peter slowly rose and walked stiffly to the kitchen door. Without knocking he entered. Eileen was cleaning the breakfast dishes. The children had gone off to school. She turned around at the noise, and there standing before her was the ghost of her lover. They stood looking at each other. Before she could speak, Peter did: "Get your things and get in the car."

Dumbly, she went upstairs, packed one bag, and came down to where Peter was waiting. After leaving a note for Andrew, she walked slowly to the car, leaving her five children, her home, her family, sat down next to a man who was nothing but skin, bones, and will, a man called "PC" whom she still did not know. Together, they drove away to a life that seemed more mysterious and more terrifying than anything she had ever known before, little realizing the worst was yet to come.

4

The Magenta Dawn Lady

The way is long, arduous, dangerous, difficult. At every step is an ambush, at every turn a pitfall. A thousand seen or unseen enemies will start up against thee, terrible in subtlety against thy ignorance, formidable in power against thy weakness. And when with pain thou hast destroyed them, other thousands will surge up to take their place. Hell will vomit its hordes to oppose and enring and wound and menace; Heaven will meet thee with its pitiless tests and its cold luminous denials.

Thou shalt find thyself alone in thy anguish, the demons furious in thy path, the Gods unwilling above thee. Ancient and powerful, cruel unvanquished and close and innumerable are the dark and dreadful Powers that profit by the reign of Night and Ignorance and would have no change and are hostile. . . . Doubtless the help is there even when it seems to be withdrawn, but still is there the appearance of total night with no sun to come and no star of hope to please in the darkness.

—Sri Aurobindo, *The Hour of God*

I didn't know what time it was. Magenta faintly streaked the horizon beyond the airbase. But it wasn't the light that I awoke to, it was the wind. Sitting in bed, I realized that I had been sweating and that the room was insufferably hot. I had stoked the coal fire before retiring—it had been a cool evening—but now it was boiling hot in my room.

Twice the entire caravan was lifted right off its blocks

by unseen hands, only to shudder into motionlessness again.

I lit a candle, slipped on my pants, and walked outside to a thick and eerie torrent of warm air. The sensuous breath of the gods whistled, hummed, rattled, and wailed in a cacophonous unending wall of sound, through fences, trees, poles, electric wires, bushes. Everything was distinctly alive, almost menacingly so.

I had been at Findhorn for one week. From Pineridge I had been moved to a caravan close to the center of the community called "The Canadian." The bed of flowers across the path was flattened to the ground in abject surrender. The near-gale-force winds gave a heroic dimension to blossoms which had previously merely looked pretty.

The noise around me increased and grew in tempo. The initial novelty had transmuted into uncertain threat, the amplitude and force made mysterious by the darkness and utter lack of clouds.

Sleep was no longer possible, so I walked the road to the Sanctuary. From outside through the gauzy curtains, I saw a soft red light glowing. Underneath sat Eileen. On her lap was a mohair rug and in her hands a blue notebook. She was writing in it.

The Sanctuary. The innermost cavity of Findhorn. Outside, the unearthly noise of a shrieking wind; inside, Eileen, pulsing, glowing red, the very heart of the organism, pumping life blood into the veins, radiating the spiritual food of the community. She was writing slowly and methodically, occasionally pausing to close her eyes, listening to that voice she has been hearing for eighteen years.

I was an interloper, an intruder into the most intimate moment in her life, a moment more sacred and profoundly personal than physical intimacy. "The exploration into God," repeatedly and rhythmically she releases and holds, surrenders and takes, listens and writes. Cosmic lovers.

I felt unwanted. I had entered where I did not belong

and could do little but stare. I could not believe what I saw, and the disbelief kept pulling and tugging, saying to get out, your disbelief is acceptable, your presence is not! The intensity of the woman held me fast. The room in which she sat seemed supercharged and electrically saturated. Her concentration alone made me feel anxious and unsettled. My nerves were bending.

Personal revelation? Facile chats with the Beloved? Small Voices? Visions of Greenhouses?

My mind was chattering away, a hungry monkey clamoring about at breakneck speed. I "knew" that Eileen was not getting "guidance" from God. In a thousand ways I "knew." And all the reasons and explanations were vying and competing with each other. The mind, full to bursting, aching with the fear of unknowing, angrily and desperately sought its lost center. The endless argument was pure intellect dancing the jig of infinite opposites. I could not experience it, I could not think it, I could not know it, I could not reason it out, how could I accept it? It was sacredly inviolate, awesomely powerful.

Suddenly, without warning, Eileen turned and looked toward me. I didn't know whether she could actually see me or not through the window, but her charcoal eyes stared directly into the darkness as if she had heard every silent word of doubt. There was no way of comprehending her expression in that moment, unless it was the unutterable loneliness and sadness of a voyager who, looking behind, sees nothing but the wake of a lifetime's journey. In that terrifying moment of her gaze, my mind was batted away like a small insect, incalculably light and hollow compared to the dense unknowing clouds before it.

The wind was funneling down the path between the Sanctuary and the Office, pressing my pants flat to my legs, sweeping my hair straight back, carrying the smells of the peninsula, the shriveled sea life lying exposed on the sand in the tide of dawn.

What happens when the conscious meets the unconscious, when the denseness of the physical meets the invisible, when the known meets the unknown? The cultural residences in the mind are slowly shaken apart by the primordial vibrations. Sound breaks glass, light cuts through steel, what does the sound and light of God do?

What happens to the mind when it begins to ask questions that only the soul can answer? The search is over, the quest complete, close the books, shut the libraries, let the air waves be still, the cortex twitches from fatigue, it has become taut, sinewy, ropy, and inflexible. Let it rest.

I really do not think she is thinking. That is the whole point. Eileen is not thinking, and I am. The distance that separates us might as well be planetary rather than the actual 20 feet.

I am beginning to suspect that everyone at Findhorn in one way or another is exploring God, and Eileen represents the ultimate earthly voyage. She will never turn back now. She is Mary the Mystic. Her knowledge of the esoteric and occult could be written on a spoon. Everything she "knows" comes from contemplative and meditative states in which she hears a voice. Those who have traveled the world mastering exotic and esoteric techniques to heighten awareness come to Findhorn and see a woman who does nothing but "sit and listen." Sit and listen. That might be the hardest one of all.

It sounds easy, but it was a lesson paid for dearly. According to mystics, when all is given to God, the mind, unprepared for the soul's journey, rebels and screams because it is unable to discern between the smaller death and the greater life. The mind goes mad, insane with fear, hate, loathing, and blackness. On the path to mystical awareness, the greatest threat to its emergence is at the threshold. Everything is stripped from the soul. It is engorged by God, and the personality falls into the void, collapses in frustrated and fearful unknowing, to burn in the fires of mutilated hope, despair, and anguish. All is surrendered; anything placed above God is ripped away. The "night" can last a single day or a lifetime. It is over when there is complete surrender, when our "greatness" is but dust before God's feet.

What are the roots that clutch, what branches grow
Out of this stony rubbish? Son of man,
You cannot say, or guess, for you know only
A heap of broken images, where the sun beats,
And the dead tree gives no shelter, the cricket no relief,
And the dry stone no sound of water. Only
There is shadow under this red rock,
(Come in under the shadow of this red rock),
And I will show you something different from either
Your shadow at morning striding behind you
Or your shadow at evening rising to meet you;
I will show you fear in a handful of dust.
                    —T. S. Eliot, The Waste Land

The wind is absolute now.

Fear is not polite, so I shall call it doubt. I doubt it.

I have learned to doubt everything.

In the magenta dawn, the red-faced, silver-haired lady-child is sitting with her head bowed down, softly sobbing, crying in the carpet piles to her God, and I doubt it.

A dog barks, and the winds howl.

Father? Father? Why aren't you going to Dublin with Auntie and me? Father? I don't want to leave you, please, Father? Oh, please, Father! Don't leave me here at the station alone with Auntie! I don't want to go to Dublin. I don't want to go to school. I don't care if I am six, Father. I want to be with you . . . Father?

The train pulled slowly out of Lucerne, Switzerland, and Eileen watched her father recede into the ironworks of the station. She was six years old, and her parents were sending her off to school. Her father would not hear of her attending schools in Egypt where they lived. Alexandria just did not have the teachers and supplies and books. She was sent to Ireland with her Aunt Florence. Florence was taking her to a "good" school where she would make lots of nice, new friends.

Friends! Eight hundred screaming friends! These are my friends, Father? Oh, Father! It is such a dreadful place, dark and dusty, reeking of coal fumes. I can't even sit in my frock, Father. It gets so black and dirty, and the children make fun of my accent. They speak so strangely, Father. I couldn't understand them, and Father, they use words that Mummy told us never to use. But everyone says them here, and they tease me because I won't, Father . . . Father, I am so lonely here. . . .

Every summer for eleven years, Eileen was sent from Alexandria, Egypt, to Dublin, Ireland—for her own good. Soon she was not alone on the trip. Her brothers and sister began to join her. She took them with her on the 4,000-mile trip, across ferries, on steamers, on trains. For five days she dutifully found them toilets, bought sandwiches and sweets at the stops, and never once did she let go of a lumpish leather bag in which were four passports and all the money. She slept with it, clutched to her breast like a teddy bear, and even at the borders passing through customs, they could not take it from her for inspection. *I am so lonely here, Father. . . .*

Peter took Eileen down to Euston Station in London. She had been here before, thirty years before, with "Auntie," and it looked much the same.

Eileen had willingly gone back to Peter. *I'll come back with you. I'll be your wife. I'll be your partner, your "other half," and cook your food, and suckle your children. But I'm putting you first, Peter. No more of this "God" business. No more of this "guidance." I don't want any of it. I am through with it. I'll be your wife, Peter. That is all.*

75

She hadn't learned the lesson. For Peter, it was no good for them simply to come back together. It had to be with God first, not himself. He had already learned that through his experience with Sheena and knew that Eileen still had to learn it. They would have to separate again until Eileen learned her lesson. Peter knew it. Sheena insisted on it. Eileen was sick at the thought of it, for they had been together for almost a year, and now Sheena decided with Peter's agreement that it was time to send her away again, this time to a summer cottage on Scotland's Isle of Mull— to be with Sheena.

It was July 1956. With her at the station was Christopher, sixteen months, and the newly born Jonathan, only six weeks old. Mull was a foreign country as far as Eileen was concerned, and she did not want to go. She had grown to despise Sheena Govan, and the thought of being with her was repulsive. *Do you really think I want to see your old wife? I have seen her enough! I have nursed her back to health again and again. I have tolerated her anger. I have suffered her biting, stinging attacks on me. I have listened patiently to her criticism of you, of the way I bring up the children, how I am not a suitable mother! I have been awakened countless times in the middle of the night to attend to her wishes, her desires. I have prayed for her, I have sat at her bed and meditated until four in the morning for her. Peter, I am terrified of her. I am so afraid of that woman. She has so much power!*

Both of the children were crying. The conductor had arranged a separate compartment for her, so she just let them cry and stared at the houses and factories passing by. It was the night train to Oban. She turned off the lights in the compartment and stepped into the aisle.

The sky was still light, and she leaned her head against the windows and let the images race past her eyes, not trying to catch them or identify them, just seeing a pattern of black shapes and dark blue patches of sky. Golden lights raced by like arrows, the sound of bells and horns rose and fell in the approach and retreat of the train, well-modulated and civilized cries absorbed in the rumble—a syncopated and soothing symphony that strangely eased her tension. Eileen felt the fatigue creeping into her bones, around her joints. Her calves ached, her arms drooped, she could actually feel the weight of each eyelid. She was tired! In the dusky light every feature was delineated—strutting jaw, high forehead and cheekbones, deep-set eyes that pierce; an even, steady look of total beingness, every nerve attuned to the one visual image in her eyes. They reflected an iron will, a light deep inside hiding itself under cultural femininity, a face of austere splendor, radiating aloofness. The fatigue brought out every tiny filigree of character and determination from her face, a face upon which is carved an innate authority.

A man who had stepped out of the adjoining compartment was staring at her. Struck by her beauty, he could not stop looking. So many have looked, have seen the perfect self-containment within the folds of the smile, a noblesse oblige that dutifully says: And here is a smile for you, young man. Her skin is paper thin, fine and smooth, and is wrapped around large round bones. There is no sign that seven children have passed through this body. She carries herself with a calm assurance and confident stillness that belies that, inside, a cauldron boils, an intense turmoil cooks in the heat of passions so strong and powerful that they frighten her, can momentarily burst the cool steely jacket of her façade and sweep the magnanimous and generous side of her character away in a flash. That inner power threatens to spill out constantly into dark areas of depression and suicidal thoughts. The fertile and procreative body could turn on itself and seek its end. The mind that cared for and loved seven siblings could lose its finely tuned grip and cross the threshold into misery. When trouble comes from without, Eileen glides through it all with an equanimity and grace as if it were nothing, a mere trifle. She oils the waters, exultantly guided by forces and allies that speak to her. But when trouble comes from within, Eileen plunges into hell.

"Oban, Oban, Oban!" The door whipped open, and a bright sword of light cut her eyes. "Oban, ma'am! Last stop!"

She sat up and squinted. It had been a miserable night's sleep. She hadn't eaten supper the night before, and now all she wanted was some coffee and breakfast. She had so little money that she pushed the thought away. She went into the waiting room to nurse Jonathan and found a dry sandwich in her purse to split with Christopher.

She opened the pram and placed Jonathan inside. Christopher was put on front, and she placed the suitcase on top. She wheeled precariously out of the train station, searching in the morning mist for the ferry to Craignure. It was a half mile away, and the fatigue of the previous evening returned full force.

The boat took an hour to reach Mull and the village of Craignure. Eileen cautiously edged down the gangway searching for a welcoming face. Someone was supposed to meet her. The pram and the children by this time had become almost intolerable. She waited until all the people had left and the ferry had pulled away. Alone again—sore, tired, and fearful. And the fear was growing. She loathed to be in Sheena's presence, and now somewhere out there Sheena was waiting for her. She didn't care how "spiritual" Sheena was supposed to be, Sheena was mean and cruel. *I won't let her lead my life, ruin my life. I'll stay a week or so, let her see the children, and then leave. She is falling apart, she is sick, she is crumbling. Peter is no longer hers! But why does she have the Power?*

She pushed the pram toward the bus station, still looking about for some sign of a friend. It was summer, but the mist and fog were cold and wet. In the unheated waiting room, Christopher began crying for food. She looked at the change in her pockets and then at the fares on the wall. There was not enough for food. She rocked Christopher in her arms and hummed into his ear, and soon all three were asleep.

The agonizing screech of steel on steel startled everyone awake. The bus to Fionaphort arrived, blowing great clouds of diesel and paraffin oil into the room. She folded up the pram and climbed aboard, at last feeling close to a destination, loathsome as it was. The bus followed a twisty narrow track, unpaved and rocky. Every window, door, seat, and handle was vibrating, shaking, twisting, and knocking as they roared around blind corners, horn blaring to unseen lorries and sheep.

The Isle of Mull. The southern part sits in a slate sea tormented by man and wind, stripped to its rocky bones, an old treeless gray fossil. It is a petrified carcass, a geological vortex of frozen magma, pierced by vertical basaltic columns like crustaceous hoarfrost monuments fallen and broken like temple ruins. Eileen's destination of Kintra sits at the foot of the brae of Druimbidh over-looking the Isle of Blackness and Isle of Storms. On the shore below, the wrack is tangled and twisted by violent tides, ripped from its hold. Like muddy and matted wool on a ram's belly, it is balled into clumps with oarweed, laver, and witchgrass, beaten into the sandy shore with its passenger shrimps and limpets until it disappears in the evening tide. Across the water the red sun dips into a horizon of storms.

The atmosphere of Mull is like a fog of thick, sea-bleached blood, vaporous and unearthly in shape, hovering above the rocks—Rocks! Black rocks, gray rocks, pink rocks, granite rocks, slate rocks, limestone rocks, coal, clay. The entire island resembles an adamantine paw whose left toenail is the blessed Isle of Iona, a neighbor sullenly envied by the native south Mullians, the Duart Clan MacLean.

COME ONE, COME ALL! BRING THE FAMILY TO DUART CASTLE, REEKING WITH DEATH AND AVARICE. SEE OUR DUNGEON CELLS, BATTLE AXES, RELIVE THE PILLAGE, THE ANCIENT SIEGES AND BURNINGS. LOOK FROM THE BATTLEMENTS THROUGH CANNON HOLES AT THE STUNNING VIEW OF BLOODY BAY, WHERE CHIEF JOHN, OUR LORD OF THE ISLES, ATTACKED HIS SON ANGUS IN GLORIOUS BATTLE. . . . ONLY 25 PENCE, V.A.T. INCLUDED.

The Clan MacLean will protest that their first eight hundred years were not spent in garroting, burning, and murder about the precincts of the isle. But when death strikes the head of the clan, the bloody past of father against son, family against family, emerges from the clan subconscious, and old fears rise again in the heart of many a clansman. For it is then that Eoghann a' Chinn will ride headless into Glen More, hurtling through the valley of desolation, claymore aglow under the misty moon with a spectral light, and above the howl of the savage winds is heard the keening cry of death.

The bus continued along a deserted stretch of abandoned lands. Great gleaming black crags thrown out from the bowels of the earth glistened as though coated with a putrescent slime. There was not a crofter or peasant or herdsman to be seen. The only croft along the way was crushed as though by some giant foot.

A car behind was honking madly, and the bus pulled over. It was the taxi that was supposed to meet Eileen. She dazedly looked at the driver and the strange passenger and just shook her head. She wasn't moving. The children were asleep, so she told the driver to meet them at Fionaphort, and on they rode through Pennyghael, Bunessan, Uisken. . .

Sheena was waiting. She was all smiles, full of good cheer, delighted to see Eileen and the children. Sheena was so kind! The cottage was full of her friends on holiday. Sheena gave Eileen a room in the back, a lean-to behind the house. There was no lighting or heating in the house. Paraffin lamps were used when needed. The toilet was an old bucket that they dumped into the ocean at low tide. The bath was made of tin, and filled from water fetched at the top of the brae behind the house.

Within a day, the tension between the two women was there again. Eileen could feel Sheena's power and spite. Her normally attractive face appeared as a grotesque mask. It was horrible to look upon, and she avoided contact with her as much as possible. The visitors left, one by one, and Sheena and Eileen were left alone.

Alone.

Alone again. A letter arrived from Peter. He had given up his job and was going to Glasgow to look for work. He wanted to know whether Eileen would mind staying on. There was no money; she would have to stay on.

Sheena began criticizing her, snapping and picking on little resentments and inconsistencies in Eileen. *Was she right? Could everything that Sheena was saying be true? Can so much hate convey even a particle of truth?*

Eileen tried to close her ears to the growing chorus of negativity. The summer cottage was becoming the last stop before hell.

Damnation! Sheena has lost Peter! She didn't want Peter! She had released Peter to marry me! Why is this witch scraping at the residue of the past, trying to unearth bits and pieces to fit her hellish puzzle?

The clamor of feverish emotions grew louder and louder, shrill voices broke into angry outbursts only to be quickly buried under blankets of mutual fear.

Sheena could not take it anymore. She decided to move out into another cottage a few miles away. She walked off . . . with Christopher.

"You are completely incapable of bringing him up. You are not worthy of this child, my dear. You are not his spiritual mother. I am his real mother! You cannot know what he means to me! You cannot know how important this

child is! My dear friend Eileen, you have lost your child. He is mine! Not yours anymore, but mine!"

Eileen remained completely expressionless. She didn't flinch but stood stock still and stared as Sheena walked up the hill with Peter's son under her arm. And it started to brew.

The cauldron came alive as never before. Fear came boiling to the top and down again in the churning stew of death. Outwardly, she seemed as impassive as this tiny island, dark and motionless. Nothing reacted, every ounce of energy was going into the fire, and the fire was up as high as she had ever felt it. The pot was red hot. Things were starting to scorch and burn. She would die soon. The fire was burning out her very insides. Her guts were scalding hot, steaming and fiery.

And then it cracked. The pot crumpled into red hot shards; the brew spilled out, setting fire to everything it touched. She was walking down the road. The bones and scraps of the past were scattered throughout her mind, seething and smoking. She walked upright and tall, erect and lone, completely alone. She walked on the sharp rocks straight toward a little granite house, straight on, staring at it, getting nearer, the heat was getting higher, everything barely contained within her, she was desperately holding the fire inside her, *I am dying. Wait just one more minute please before I die!* Step by step, closer, closer to that door, the green door on the pink granite house with the light in the window. *Sheena is home! Thirty more seconds, I need thirty more.* CLUMP CLUMP CLUMP across the thick turf. *She can hear nothing can she, she doesn't know I'm coming, wait, wait, wait, waaaiiittt!!!!!*

Sheena was sitting and writing a letter to Peter, telling him how she felt Eileen wasn't in a fit state to look after Christopher, and how it would be best for all concerned if she kept the dear thing, the sweet little thing. *Peter will understand. He always understands these matters, and he trusts me. Peter is so faithful. He is like a puppy dog! Good-*

natured and naïve. Once a friend of Peter's, there is noth-
ing in the world he won't do for you. The friends legends
are made of. If I told him to fly to the moon he would at
least make a serious attempt. What a grand and dear friend
he has been, and he has learned so much. I always knew
the marriage was temporary, only a means to an end. Did
he not know it too? No, of course not. How could he know?
He trusts everyone so completely and implicitly. I know
he will understand about this little thing with Christopher.
Eileen is in such a state now. She just can't handle the two
children. She needs a rest. A time of inner searching and
fulfillment. She will see that I was right again. . . .

Sheena was lost in her thoughts and didn't hear the front
door open. She looked up, and her whole body froze into
one long eternal moment of horror. Shock, fear, and terror
suffused every fiber and cell of her being.

She did not know what hit her.

A torrent of words spewed and slopped over, spilled and
burned. Burrowing pain. Deeper and deeper, she felt all
the spite and envy that she had thrown out at Eileen for
the past two years as a rank and putrid garbage that had
been cooked down to a vile-tasting stuff and was now being
poured down her gullet. Every last bit was coming back,
and she was helpless. She couldn't bear to look or hear any
longer; the crackling roar of destruction issued forth from
the demon's maw of fire, revealing charred sinewy cords
of flesh that had once covered her rotten and bitter life.
It was herself she was seeing pressed into a few minutes of
pure, unadulterated, flaming hatred, and it almost killed
her.

A few days later, Sheena quietly left the island, slipping
off with Christopher, leaving Eileen with Jonathan. Eileen
received another letter from Peter. He was in Glasgow,
had a temporary job selling Kleen-Eze brushes door to
door, and was living at a Bed and Breakfast.

The row with Sheena left Eileen empty, drained, and

exhausted. But there was still the fear and the dread. She had merely taken all the spite Sheena had piled upon her and returned it.

Autumn came, but there were no trees to mark its passage. Nothing fell to the ground except rain and tattered pieces of wool from the sheep. Winds borne by the mountains' icy breath blew in, alternating with the rain driven by the Atlantic storms. Rain and cold.

The once-a-year supply of coal was gone. There were great piles of it next door, but the suspicious and grim-looking neighbors would just stare at Eileen as if she were a freak. Never once did any one of the several people in the collection of six houses so much as say one word to her. She was English, she had something to do with that weird Govan woman. Stay away from her—she is bad!

Eileen's letters to Peter grew hardened and bitter. The cold put her nerves on edge. The dampness began to seep in and sit with her through the night. The midsummer light had given way to the long nights of darkness. The wind began to blow; her food was almost gone: a few potatoes, some crackers, and some flour.

As the days became shorter, the sun barely tipped over the ridge. The cold and dampness increased. The fear she felt at her situation began to eat away at what little reserves she had. The sixteen-hour nights became intolerably cold, black, and empty. During the day she would walk about looking for scraps of peat along the road, but now even this precious fuel had run out. Somebody had left some watercolors behind in the cottage. She tried to paint a picture but found her hands so cold that she couldn't hold the brush.

TAP. . . . TAP. . . . TAP!

She looked up at the frosty windows. Who on earth would come at night to see her? Was it the wind?

TAP. . . . TAP. . . . TAP!

She held Jonathan close.

"Yes?"

The door opened a crack and then seemed to hang there. Somebody was there but wouldn't come in. She could hear the heavy breathing.

"Yes?" she repeated.

The door opened another inch, and she could see the dirty face of a young man. His mouth was hanging open, the teeth were all crooked, some were missing.

"Come in, please," she said firmly.

The door opened another foot, and she could see that it was the village simpleton who lived with his father and mother up the road. He smiled; a crude and ungainly gap split his face. He was acutely embarrassed, but also rather bold and unchecked.

"Yes? . . . Is there something . . .?"

He ambled awkwardly into the room, a rude hulking figure in a dirty and dung-encrusted tweed coat, his cap off to a rakish angle as if someone had put it on him in the morning and had forgotten to tell him. The trousers were decidedly too big for him, rolled up into huge boats of cuffs at the bottom, exposing thick woolen socks that had been worn so often that they fell limply over the tops of his shoes.

He looked at her for a long time, as if he had forgotten for a minute what it was he had come for. A slight shiver of doubt ran through Eileen. She was alone. What had he come for? He was a simpleton, but he had desires, he was a man. . . . She tried to put away those thoughts.

He moved one more awkward step into the room and closer to Eileen. He reached into his bulging pockets, with big, blackened hands, hands covered with cracks, dirt, straw, dung, coal, and three-day-old porridge. One by one, he took out pieces of peat and set them on the table. With each piece he looked at Eileen with a timorous expectancy as if he had just laid at her feet the jewels and gold of the kingdom.

She knew then she had a friend. One real friend. After depositing the peat on the wooden table, he slowly reached into the other pocket. Bread! An apple! A lump of butter in an oil-soaked newspaper! Grinning anxiously, he reached for one last item. He couldn't find it. Where was it? He grabbed and tugged at his pocket, and his face changed from a smile to one of pain, a little child's look of surprise and shock and wonder undercut by disappointment. His hand slowly withdrew. It was covered with a shiny substance that dripped on the floor. At the lip of his pocket was a brown piece of eggshell.

Eileen carefully washed his pocket and hands. When he had left, after playing some Highland airs on his mouth organ, Eileen was overwhelmed by the irony of the situation. Her only friend in life. Peter had been a friend, but he was gone. He was under the influence of Sheena and had abandoned her. Her family had severed ties after she left Andrew. Her children were secreted away. Her mother and father were dead. Even her brother and sister whom she had carefully ferried to Egypt were now afraid to talk to her. Christopher was with Sheena. There was no one except this one simple and beautiful little idiot! And that realization almost crushed her.

She hadn't talked to anyone for months, and soon she was talking to herself, in a long, maniacal drone. She didn't know whether she was talking aloud or not, and it didn't matter because there was no one to listen. . . . *I hate God, I hate Sheena, I hate this hellhole, God, why have you done this to me? Take my last child, take him! Take him! I want to die on those rocks by the shore, but take my child first, I won't leave him. Oh! he is the seventh son! Oh! miserable son, you were to be the blessed and lucky one, you wretched poor little thing. I won't leave you, that is the only thing I can't do, but I can't stay any longer, God, I must go, it is over, and now I must leave. . . . Oh! God take him! Someone take this queer little soul clinging to*

*my breast ... take him! ... Peter is gone! ... Will I ever
see him again? Andrew is gone ... the children are gone
... Sheena is gone ... Christopher is gone ... Oh! where
is Dorothy now? ... Father is dead ... It is so alone,
Father ... and Mother is dead ... the coal is gone, where
did I put that piece of peat? ... the heat is gone ... the
cold is here, God ... and the wind is here ... why are you
here, wind? ... the wind is here, God, right in this room,
and I don't know how it got in ... it is so cold ... it ...
is ... lonely ... do you want me, God? ... You have
everything now ... There is nothing I can give you save
Jonathan ... You will have to take him ... Take him ...
go ahead ... if you must, take him ... but I won't let go
... I am so lonely here, Father. ...*

The record played on and on, day after day, night after
sleepless nightmare-filled night. The cold. The hunger.
Food would come down the hill late at night in the basket
of a bicycle ridden by an idiot. Even he didn't dare to be
seen with this woman. He was smart enough to know that.

Eileen was dying, a death filled with grotesque visions,
each more horrible than the last. They passed before her
eyes, stray thoughts like vicious animals leaping out every
moment. Her body and soul screamed out for love, warmth,
a smile, any sign of affection. ...

A great buzzard flew overhead. A sheep had died during
the night. Everything she saw confirmed those inner visions
—a gray violent ocean, the frozen water in the sink, purple
hands, a baby's endless howling, tiny ivory teeth of rats
nibbling under her bed at night. Bitter scowls on the faces
of the shriveled and miserable crofters. ...

*There is something outside the door! I hear a noise. No,
there isn't. It's not outside. It is inside. It is here ... it's
gone again ... no! there it is again ... it is a voice. Listen!
It is a voice. It murmurs and whispers and then.... LISTEN!
... It comes between the thoughts, slipping in again and
again, a voice now louder and growing, I can hear it. ...*

LISTEN! . . . PUT ME FIRST IN EVERYTHING, THEN SHALL ALL
BE ADDED UNTO YOU. . . . LISTEN! . . . BE AT PEACE. STRIVING
GETS YOU NOWHERE. IT SIMPLY LEAVES YOU EXHAUSTED AND
FRUSTRATED BECAUSE YOU NEVER SEEM TO BE NEARER THE
GOAL. JUST LEARN TO BE. WHEN YOU HAVE CEASED STRIVING,
CRAWL INTO MY LOVING ARMS LIKE A WEARY CHILD. EN-
CIRCLED IN THOSE ARMS, FEEL THE PEACE, COMFORT, AND
COMPLETE ONENESS WITH ME. FEEL YOURSELF MELT INTO
ME. . . .

Gently and persistently, the voice grew in her heart,
pushing out the thoughts, turning off the record.

LISTEN! . . . WALK MY WAY AND DO MY WILL. LET ME SHOW
YOU MY WONDERS AND GLORIES. IF YOU SEEK HAPPINESS IN
THE WRONG WAY, IT CANNOT BE FOUND. SEEK ME FIRST AND
FIND ME. THAT IS THE SIMPLE ANSWER. PUT FIRST THINGS
FIRST, NO MATTER WHAT THE COST OR SACRIFICE. LOVE ME
WITH ALL YOUR HEART, WITH ALL YOUR SOUL, AND ALL YOUR
MIND.

The mind which had been twisted on the racks of self-
torture ceased its mighty resistance. The stretching anxiety
and pain eased and abated. Her body, which had become
hard and knotted, relaxed its tense grip on nothingness.
From the moment she had arrived on Mull, her "guidance"
had been cut off. Now, as if she were floating in a pool of
water, a warm and soothing impulse began to wash over
her, cleansing her, purifying her. She let go of everything.
Her body no longer felt cold and hungry. Her emotions,
raw and seared, were finally played out. In and outside the
house was a complete and utter stillness and peace. She
accepted everything. She was a frail and tired woman who
needed love. Her brother and sister were still her family.
Peter was her partner, her mate, and her lover, and he was
real and beautiful. The whole of her life seemed perfect
and one.

It was early in the morning. She looked at the calendar
and saw it was Christmas Day. Christmas! She smiled at

the joke God was playing on her. She put on her sweater and walked outside to a wintry sun. The water in the sound was sparkling blue, and the wind was raising white caps on the surface. It streamed through her hair and clothes like the gentle breath of God. It was no longer cold, it was no longer a threat, it was God as surely as everything around her was God—the ocean smells, the crying seagulls winging in circles overhead, the pebbles under her feet, the bleating of the sheep, and even those huge massive granite rocks around the house. And God was smiling.

"Good morning, Mrs. Caddy. A fine day, isn't it now?" She wheeled around toward this strange voice. It was her neighbor. He was looking at her with glowing eyes and a wide toothsome grin. Eileen's face began to move uncontrollably, and she managed to say, "*Oh, yes*," and without stopping walked toward the point and the water's edge.

It was a great gleaming blue circus tent of a sky. The wind blew sharply near the shore. It roared in her ears. *For the first time, I could weep, not with sadness or not even joy, but just cry to God, and salt came out of my eyes and salt spray washed my face and hair, and the tears and the ocean knew each other, and I was with Peter and we were one. . . .*

In the distance through the sparkling water in her eyes, she could see Iona, the Isle of Peace. She could see the Abbey and wondered if the bells would be ringing a Christmas Mass. Even in the winter the isle was green, glowing, and awesome.

She knew! She suddenly knew! With all her heart she knew! Peter was coming! And she ran with the wind back to the house and there stood Peter, a Christmas chicken hanging from one hand, the other outstretched to Eileen. He was smiling and laughing, with a look in his eyes that seemed to say: *I've been waiting, we've been waiting, you've been so alone. . . .*

The Hollow

Bisto for Gravies, Margett's Raspberry Fruit Flan Fillings, Samuel Down's Pigeon Blend Whiskey, Fowler's West India Treacle, Nell Gwynn Marmalade, Bird's Family Size Custard Powder, Bisto for Gravies, Walker's Famous Highland Shortbread, MacVities's Gypsy Creams, Ambrosia Rice Pudding, Baxter's Sweet and Tender Baby Beets in Vinegar, Bisto for Brown Gravies, Cadbury's Assorted Biscuits in Butterfly Lacquered Tins, Cruickshank's Lime Crush, and Bisto . . . for Thick Brown Gravies.

Eileen stared. *A moldy golf shoe, mattress springs, barbed wire, oil drums, three pistons, a rotting steamer trunk, rusty Flexa mower wheels, a sun-bleached hot water bottle, and . . . Bisto for the thickest, richest gravies around.*

Eileen stood at the edge of a rubbish heap which was to be her new home. But she could not believe it. She had received guidance that this was where she, Peter, and the three children were to move, and yet she could not believe it. Bisto for Gravies!

Peter and Eileen left Mull and settled in Glasgow. They lived in a rooming house while Peter worked around at odd jobs. A "chance" interview landed him a position as manager of the Cluny Hill, a large, luxury hotel in the north of Scotland at Forres, four miles from the village of Findhorn. Dorothy Maclean had quit her job in London and came up to join them as Peter's secretary.

Peter knew little in fact about running a hotel, and even less about a large one employing a staff of fifty. He didn't know how much to pay them, whom to engage for what services, or even how much to charge the guests.

Whenever in doubt, Peter will seek out an expert and pick his brains. Seeing no one among the staff around who possessed management experience, he did the next best thing—he asked God. Peter decided that he alone couldn't run and operate a hotel, so he turned the job over to his longtime associate and companion. After all, it was His Plan, wasn't it?

Every single question about the running of the hotel was submitted to Eileen, who received the answers in guidance. No matter what time of day, no matter what the circumstance, Eileen had to drop everything, sit quietly, meditate, and hear The Voice. She could be up to her ears in dirty nappies, and Peter would burst in demanding immediate attention, as he did one night when the cook on duty was babbling drunk in the kitchen just before the big Saturday night dinner. The cook was staggering around the kitchen, demanding another glass of whiskey before he would so much as touch an onion. The dining room was filling rapidly, the hors d'oeuvres were being served, and he was bellowing for more whiskey. Eileen sat down with pen and notebook, listened for a moment, and wrote: "Tell Peter to give him another whiskey." Peter looked astonished, took the piece of paper, and read it over and over as he walked to the bar. He poured a measure of whiskey and strode into the kitchen and put it in the shaking hand of his astonished cook. The evening meal went off without a hitch.

Most hotels treated their staff as disposables, something you throw away at the end of the season, usually providing

them with small, cramped quarters, since they were occupied only during the summer months. Peter, Eileen, and
Dorothy were guided to do it differently. They created a
family feeling within the staff. Everyone was treated with
respect. Dorothy painted the staff quarters at the beginning
of the season and polished the floors until they shone.
Eileen placed flowers in each of the rooms. The staff members were treated as well as the guests, and like the clientele
that Peter was building, they returned year after year.

What had once been a marginal hotel now trebled its
receipts and was promoted to four-star rating. Their success
startled everyone, and Peter and Eileen began to assume
some social stature in the surrounding community. However, stories of how the hotel was run on God's guidance
and rumors of the Caddys' spiritual activities began to
circulate. The national press wrote a story about the Cluny
Hill and called it the "Heavenly Hotel."

The owners were pleased with the income and receipts,
but they were uncomfortable with this maverick manager
who attracted so much attention and unwanted publicity.
The company owned another twenty hotels, and one of
them, the Trossachs near Glasgow, nicknamed the "graveyard of managers," was rapidly fading and losing large
sums of money. Having tried innovations similar to those
that Peter had instituted at Cluny Hill without success,
they solved both problems by ordering Peter to leave the
Cluny and manage the Trossachs—no more rumors
in Forres and someone to revive the worst of their
hotels.

With twenty-five of the original Cluny Hill staff, Peter
and Eileen reluctantly made the move from Forres to Loch
Katrine, obeying only because of Eileen's guidance which
cryptically announced "that many lessons were to be
learned at the Trossachs."

Peter poured his energies into the place, using every
technique of positive thinking he had learned. His pro-

phetic cook, still with them after five years, leaned over to Peter with a dense whiskey-filled breath and said, "You won't change it! The evil is in the very bricks of the place, and you won't be able to get it out!" Up until then, every one of the prescient utterances had come true.

Struggle and work as they might, they found it impossible to instill a spirit of love and joy into the place. Blackness and evil did indeed seem to permeate it, and its location in the rainiest spot in Scotland did little to help matters. The Graveyard of Managers. There was dissension and drinking among the staff, some of whom were bitter at having to leave the Cluny Hill and wanted to return. Some left; others sulked and quarreled. The place had a depressing effect on everyone.

Toward the end of the first season, Peter wrote to the management of the company requesting a transfer to the Cluny Hill and emphasizing that he could not ask his staff to remain at the Trossachs another year. He received no reply and wrote again, inviting them to visit and discuss the situation. Nothing happened. On the morning of the last day of the season, Eileen received guidance that one of the lessons for the New Age to be learned at the Trossachs was absolute flexibility. And sure enough, Peter walked out of the room after listening to that little tidbit of advice to find a pink slip and an army of "stocktakers" counting every last fork and pillowcase, combing the place for losses or thefts. Although nothing was found amiss, Peter was asked to leave within four hours. The Outrageous Flexible Plan. Having devoted six years of their lives to the company, working without holidays day in and day out, week after week, year after year, from early in the morning to past midnight, they found the decision absolutely bewildering. No reason for the abrupt dismissal was given.

They had no place to go except the old caravan they had left on the beach at Findhorn. The boys were gathered from school, everything was hastily packed, and in confusion and doubt, they left early in the afternoon. Peter asked Eileen to get guidance, and it said that they had learned enough lessons at the Trossachs and that they were to be grateful to the company because it was playing an important role in God's plan. That, of course, confused them even more.

They arrived at the beach near Findhorn overlooking the Moray Firth. The fresh air and scenery did much to soothe their outraged feelings, and while the children played outside, Peter and Eileen recuperated and counted their losses. They had no money, no job, no home, and nowhere to go.

The village of Findhorn had strict ordinances prohibiting caravans from remaining on the beach past the summer months. It was already October, and the sanitary inspector was insisting that they move on. When they realized that the only other place in the area that would accept caravans was the Findhorn Bay Caravan Park, memories returned of the times when they had driven by, taking guests to the yacht club, gesturing with a disdainful flourish and saying: "Imagine living in a dump like that, cheek by jowl next to each other." They kept putting off the inspector, desperately seeking some alternative, but finally, in November, they knew that they had to go there, if only for a short time.

Peter selected a site away from the other caravans, located in the bottom of a hollow between sandy slopes of gorse, broom, and grass. The caravan park was surrounded on three sides by water, and the ocean-born winds caused the sand to shift and move around the site. Bleak as it was, the surrounding dunes offered protection from the wintry storms and a measure of privacy as well. In the middle of the hollow was an old garage which Peter rented from the site owner.

On the morning of November 16, 1962, Peter hitched

up his caravan. Jonathan, who was ill at the time, remained in his bed, while they slowly convoyed the mile from the beach to the caravan site. Eileen was deeply troubled by the turn of events, worrying and fretting that Peter, now middle-aged and jobless, might fall apart and become demoralized. The prospect of moving from the beach to the caravan site seemed to be a sign that their life was deteriorating. That morning, the first storm of winter moved in, bringing gray skies and bitter cold. When they approached the site, she was overcome with dread. The garage which Peter had rented had been damaged by vandals. The doors hung limply by their hinges, banging in the gusty winds. Glass was strewn about the site, every window having been broken.

It began to snow.

Eileen stared. Next to the site was something Peter hadn't told her about. It was the local dump, rotting and stinking with garbage, rusted bedsprings, bald tires, broken bottles, tin cans, mattress ticking blown about like dirty patches of snow, and rusty encrusted cans of Bisto.

The guidance seemed ridiculous. From the prestigious post of hotel manager, Peter had been reduced to humiliating and degrading circumstances. As he squinted out of caravan windows at a rubbish dump, he wistfully remembered the magnificent green valley he once saw from his four-room suite at the Cluny Hill. From his handsomely paid former position, he was reduced to living on eight pounds a week unemployment benefits. His faith and obedience to Eileen's guidance brought him scorn; his former colleagues pretended not to know him; his friends abandoned him in droves. After trying to find another job immediately, but being "mysteriously" blocked in every attempt, he was told through guidance to wait and live in the moment.

Just accept what is happening. Know that I would not let anything happen to you, for you are all precious to Me.

All that you have undergone in the past has led you up to this. You cannot understand now why I have laid my hand on you of all people. Let this not perturb you. One day, you will know, but now there is much that you have to accept in faith. . . . There is a clear pattern running through all that has been happening to you. What appears as great misfortune is the most wonderful blessing.

Peter had worked in a world of priorities, schedules, orders, and planning. Life was *planned*, and those who did not submit to this suffered the consequences. In the military environment of graphs, projections, printouts, stages, degrees, and ranks, the fellow who got ahead lived a life of order and precision. His arrangements for catering to large masses of mobile airmen were masterpieces of analysis and administration. But in the hollow, Peter was asked to abandon and relinquish planning and to accept the full implications of living in the moment, not knowing where the next meal or shilling was coming from. Despite the outward turn of events, Peter's rocklike faith in Eileen's guidance remained undiminished. He knew there was no security to be sought, and that their real security could rest only in their faith in God.

Eileen's guidance began to unfold a tale as mysterious as it was fantastic, a story of the future that was tantalizing in its hints of what was to come, yet straightforward and sincere in its warnings of the difficulties that lay ahead. Peter and Eileen stepped over into an existence that was dreary and depressing in form yet mythical in vision. The guidance spoke of a time when thousands of people would come to that place to join together as a larger whole, to preserve and enlarge the beauty and communion that was humanity, to form through love an integrated and whole community, a "city of light" on a planet that was disintegrating into violence and despair. They were to be an island of light in a sea of darkness.

When it became obvious that they were there to stay, an annex was built onto their caravan for Dorothy Maclean.

The original caravan measured 9 by 32 feet, and Dorothy's room added another 10-by-10-foot space. Into the whole were squeezed two bedrooms, a kitchen, a bathroom and toilet, and a living room which doubled as bedroom and dining room. During that winter, in the hardship of accommodating three adults and three lively boys in such a small space, they all experienced what it means to live in harmony and, conversely, what hell it is not to. Corners of personalities were chipped off, tensions became fairly thick, but slowly they learned how to blend their consciousnesses into a greater whole and to act and work as a group.

Christmas and New Year's Day rolled by, and they remained in their tiny trailer, rocked and shaken by the winds that swept over the dunes. Although the hollow afforded some protection, it was not enough to prevent sand and dirt from whirling around the site. The wind would howl and race, and every time one of the children opened the caravan door, sand poured into the room.

The winter was spent in reading and contemplation, since the weather completely prevented any outdoor activities. In spite of her guidance, Eileen hoped that they would return to their old jobs at the Cluny Hill Hotel, but when they went on welfare, her hopes sank. She felt ashamed and humiliated. She no longer left the caravan site at all, not even to go to the shop a couple of hundred yards away.

There are two distinct aspects of Eileen. One, born and bred middle class, is accustomed to the amenities of life and sensitive to the mores and standards of that class. This Eileen suffered constantly and almost had a mental breakdown. But there is another part to Eileen, one which may be called the phenomenal Eileen, one which she does not completely identify with, even today. This is an Eileen who can sit down and withdraw into a deep and prolonged meditative state in which there is complete peace and relaxation. It is as if she were another person at whom she looks rather dispassionately yet with complete respect.

In stillness she would hear a voice as clearly as any, a

voice giving her distinct messages which she would write down, but she refused to fully accept these words.

It was Peter rather than Eileen who had a good idea what this voice was and what it meant—it was nothing less than God. He had absolute faith in these messages and never questioned for a moment their origin. Not feeling the necessity to analyze the "whys" and "wherefores," Peter unwaveringly obeyed the pronouncements, acting upon each immediately and swiftly. The training had become intricately and strongly interlinked with the guidance, so that if a message was received that something was to be done, as far as Peter was concerned it was so, and he would act upon it immediately.

Eileen, on the other hand, thought psychics, mediums, and sensitives to be a dubious lot with whom she did not care to associate, and felt shaky about the whole business. Her strictly orthodox Church of England upbringing talked about an enshrined God of the scriptures whose hand was in everything, but a God separated from man. You didn't talk to Him, and He certainly didn't talk to you. Eileen did not want to be a sensitive unconsciously projecting her desires through the medium of "revelation." She was determined to refuse this impulse with all her strength, but try as she would, she could not resist the call to sit and listen.

Yet during that first winter, her deeper doubts surfaced in the form of negativity and complaints. The faith that had been built up through their successful operation of the Cluny Hill was shattered by the abysmal living conditions she found herself in, for she could not reconcile this with the positive and almost cheerful guidance which repeatedly said "All is well."

Peter could easily accept the difficult living conditions, the poverty, the coldness, and hardship, but he could not accept Eileen's doubts and negativity. He began to give Eileen the same training that he had received as a youth from Dr. Sullivan, training in positive thinking. And Peter is probably one of the world's foremost exponents of positive thinking, in theory and practice—his supercharged approach to life makes Dale Carnegie look like a cowering beggar in comparison. Nothing is insurmountable. As far as Peter is concerned, there is nothing that he cannot do providing it has God's stamp of approval. Peter taught Eileen that life and thought are inseparable and any distinction between the two is artificial, that we are what we think, and what we think becomes what we are and everything around us. If Eileen dwelt on negativity then she would create the very thing she feared. It seemed to work, for soon the complaining ceased and Eileen's faith bloomed anew.

Let not your heart be troubled. You believe in Me. Trust in Me. Allow no doubts or fears to enter. Let yourself be used as My channel to radiate My love at all times. Step out of that mist of despondency into pure light where all is clear and beauty surrounds you. . . . Start the day with a loving positive thought, and you will find that the day is bound to be different. You lead such a sheltered and secluded life. You are inclined to forget the way that millions live in the big cities, the hustle and bustle, the rat race, the dirt and squalor. It is good to remember this, because it will fill your heart with deep gratitude that I have led you to this life where peace and beauty surround you, where the air is pure and the living is simple. You are mightily blessed. Accept these blessings, stretch out and do my work, and let My peace and love be yours at all times, gifts from Me, your heavenly Father. Always go with My guidance and never against it. It is when you go against it that trouble starts. I am very patient and very loving and keep on showing you the way. But it is up to you to take it. I can only show you—the action must be yours. You are not living as individuals but as a group. Therefore you can find perfect unity only if you seek My will. It will be a very thrilling and exciting life for all of you, but you must stay close to Me and not try to run things your way.

Eileen's increased faith prompted a desire to meditate for longer periods of time, but with six people in the caravan bumping into each other moving from room to room, there was hardly any quiet or a place to be alone. Late one night, having asked in meditation where she might find some peace and quiet, she received an immediate response which made her wish she hadn't asked: *Go down to the public toilets and have your time of quiet there.* It would have been more humorous if she didn't have to do it, but if that was what the Good Lord wanted her to do, then she was going to do it, so she put her notebook and pencils into a bag, bundled up in a thick coat, and walked through the freezing night to the public toilet, where she sat, night after night, until the early hours of the morning. Inside the odoriferous and unheated building with its wire mesh windows, she might as well have been sitting on a fence post for all the protection it afforded from the elements. But there she came every night for the first winter and for five years following, never missing a night, having visions and hearing the Voice, realizing and relearning three to five hours a night that God was everywhere for He was within.

That first winter was one of those long and unusually cold ones that seem to recur every eleven years along with sunspots and droughts. For three months, their caravan was covered with ice, freezing all the pipes, making it necessary to bring in their water from a tap down the road. Their walks with buckets of water became a pantomime of studied action as they navigated the frozen sheets of ice that covered everything.

With the approach of Easter and the spring thaw, Peter looked out from his living room door to the grass-covered hillock with an eye toward improvement. Eileen received in guidance that they were to build a patio which would protect them from the winds when they sat outside, at the same time preventing sand from coming into the caravan. With no money available for concrete, they acted in faith and collected stones for the bed. When they were finished and ready for the concrete, a neighbor came by and told them that several tons of damaged cement had just been dumped by the side of the road outside the gate. Finding exactly what they needed by the road, they were able to finish the patio within a few days. Peter next turned his attention to the ground adjacent to it, a sandy patch partially shaded by the fence, and thought it would be suitable for lettuce and radishes.

Although Peter had absolutely no experience with gardening, he had spent the winter reading about Bio-Dynamic and organic methods of horticulture. All of those books presumed you had soil, but when Peter examined his "soil," he discovered it was a light, powdery sand with no organic matter or water retention qualities whatsoever. Peter's dilemma was compounded by his utter lack of resources; he was flat broke, and he couldn't buy peat, manure, compost, or good tools.

Peter did the only thing he could do. He removed the turflike grass that covered the sand and dug a trench a foot and a half wide and a foot deep. Into the bottom of the trench he placed the turf upside down and broke it up with a spade. On top of this he replaced the sand and then sowed the seeds. Because the ground was devoid of organic material, he watered the beds every day by hand.

Between the patio and the garage was another piece of ground measuring eight by ten feet which Peter decided to tackle in the same way, this time with the addition of horse manure which was given to him by a local stable owner. Around this patch a wire fence was built to keep the rabbits out, and inside were planted peas, runner beans, carrots, beets, and more lettuce.

Peter still had in the back of his mind that he ought

to get a job, but when the attempts continued to be "strangely" thwarted, he started on the piece of ground behind the garage on the opposite side of the caravan from the patio. He wanted to build a compost heap there, but had run out of manure from the stable owner. While driving to get straw one day, he gave a lift to a man who, having just placed his three horses in a field adjacent to the caravan park, told Peter that he was welcome to the manure if he could use it. Peter unhesitatingly accepted. The next day, he went to the field with Dorothy and Eileen to make good on the offer and found that they were the object of astonished looks as passing motorists slowed their pace and gawked at the three adults wandering in the pasture, buckets and shovels in hand, scooping up manure under the patient gaze of the horses.

Dorothy and Eileen's job was to collect seaweed, which they cut off the rocks at low tide in the afternoons before the children returned from school. On one particularly cold day, when both were standing up to their knees in water, Eileen's hand slipped and the knife slashed her palm. She and Dorothy looked in horror at the gash, and then Eileen quickly closed her hand and prayed in a whisper, "I affirm wholeness," over and over. Finally she looked up and opened her hand, and Dorothy saw that it was clean and unblemished. There was not even a mark. They said nothing, but continued to work—in awe.

As the weather improved, Peter took long walks through the moors along the ocean side of the peninsula. From the roll-and-tumble terrain, undulant like the sea around it, springs forth a tough and spiny grass, two to three feet long, which grows in tight clumps and holds the sand in place, giving the landscape a herringbone appearance of grasses interlaced and crisscrossed. In all weather and at all times, there is the wind, blowing in from the sea, dancing about the moor in sun and rain, snow or mist, bringing with it a tingling briny smell, a pure cleansing bath of air which has molded the entire landscape.

Away from the wind and back toward home, Peter turned, breathing in the heady odor of the yellow gorse blossoms. In the setting sun, the delicate flowers looked like golden pennies stuck fast to thorny crowns, while beneath and all about him large gray rabbits scurried into holes. Peter heard a strange bleating across the rise. When he reached the top he could see a white object tossing and turning. It was a sheep, hanging upside down, entangled in a barb wire fence, unable to escape. Peter carefully sorted out the wires and freed it. Its legs had been wounded, but before he could fully check its condition, it bolted away to join the rest of its flock. Thinking that the sheep might need attention, Peter walked to the farmer's house to inform him of what he had done. In gratitude, the farmer gave them a load of manure which he personally delivered to the caravan site the next day.

To the compost pile Peter added peat dross and cummings, a barley residue that is thrown out by the malting companies. One of the shopkeepers in town, noticing that the Caddys would buy only the least expensive vegetables and fruits, remembered when they were his very good customers at the Cluny Hill and began to give them all his spoiled vegetables, particularly potatoes, of which he always had a fair amount. Peter and Eileen would carefully pick through the potatoes, put aside sound parts that were not completely rotten, and use them to make potato soup, which became their nightly staple. The overripe bananas that could be rescued were mashed up with milk for dessert. The remaining produce was added to the compost piles.

All their needs were being met, simply and gracefully.

Why should not your every need be met? Are you not My children and have I not laid My hand on you? Believe that all things are possible, and make them so. There is no storing away for a rainy day. Therefore, never hoard anything. Whatever you have, use as a gift from Me, and know there is plenty more where that came from. Remember this, and you'll cease looking ahead and cease looking back. You will live to the full now. As your needs are met, give constant thanks.

Their new diet was a relief from hotelier's fare. At the Cluny Hill, Peter and Eileen had set the tone and example and consequently ate the same food as the guests, five- and six-course meals with a bottle of wine and a brandy to round it off. At the Hollow, their diet became exceedingly simple. *You will find that as your bodies become more and more refined, your intake of solid foodstuffs will diminish. You will begin to absorb nourishment from the sun and fresh air as your bodies get rid of impurities.* Peter was told to run on the beach and swim when not working in the garden. A schedule evolved in which he stopped work before lunch and dinner and ran three or four miles along the water's edge before diving into the icy sea.

The guidance informed them that they would live almost completely on what was produced from their garden and that this was important, because this food contained vibrations that were more refined than the foods obtained in town. Their diet consisted almost entirely of vegetables, salads, fruits, wheat germ, bread, and honey. Eileen had been told to eliminate red meat from their diet and shortly thereafter white meat as well. *This refining of your bodies is a slow process, and I do not ask you to do anything drastic. Gradually get used to absorbing vegetables and fruits into your system. Your systems will become quite accustomed to them and will not crave anything more. Know too that all you are doing, whether it is the food you eat, the work you do, the sunshine and fresh air that you absorb, the harmony you work in—all are carrying you ever further into the New. The Old is finished. Tell Peter that all the work that he is putting into this place will bear vegetables in abundance. He is making this a very special place. It is to be used tremendously in the days ahead.*

Peter's activity in the garden increased until he was

working from early in the morning until late at night. All the necessary materials for compost had been gathered and collected except for the straw needed to cover and protect it. On the day the piles were ready, a neighbor brought them a bale that he had found alongside the road. Peter's every need for the garden was manifested at just the right time so that not a day was lost in waiting. The same neighbor, realizing that they needed wood, offered old lumber from buildings he was dismantling in exchange for Peter's help in carting it away. The wood was used to enlarge the garden by building pathways, cold frames, and fences. Peter then moved to a new patch of ground just north of the compost piles onto which were planted leeks, celery, rutabagas, turnips, peas, beans, and more radishes and lettuce. The first piece of ground was already bearing lettuce and radishes, and the carrots were just starting to be thinned. Everybody, even the children, was pouring energy into the garden.

Although there was no income except National Assistance, they lacked for nothing, feeling showered with God's blessings as if they were in a very special place, an oasis of peace surrounded by what was becoming a lovely garden. Instead of resentment or bitterness, there emerged an appreciation for all that was free: the brilliant sunshine, the sea air, the purest water, fresh natural vegetables from their garden, the romps on the beach, and the varied and spectacular sunsets of the northern skies.

Repeatedly, Eileen received guidance that the process of growing their own food was a step toward a new body, a new spirit, and a new life. *What you are eating now is doing far more good than any other food you've eaten in your lives. You are to try to remember that you are in the process of preparing your bodies for something quite new. Therefore, what your eating habits were in the past do not come into the picture. This is the New. Therefore, you will find that you are capable of completely new habits, new ways of thinking. All the old ruts and molds are to be destroyed. You are not to go by anything you have read in a book regarding diet. The more food your body absorbs from the garden the better. You have to gradually refine your body. As it becomes finer and less dense your skin will begin to be able to absorb substances which at present it is incapable of doing. It is as if layer after layer of old skin has to be peeled off, leaving only the fine layer which can absorb these purities from the ethers. You will find that your body will know what it can absorb and what is good and bad for it, and you will eat things instinctively. The old must go, and the quicker you realize this and do something about it the better. I want you to realize that the produce out of this garden has tremendous life force and will do you more good than anything bought. This food is blessed. Absorb it and be ever grateful.*

The garden became a focal point in their lives and by May passers-by could notice something different and special about it: everything was higher, larger, greener, and more vibrant than any they had seen before. At this point Peter received guidance from Eileen that he was to plant everything that would grow there, plantings which would ultimately embrace sixty-five different vegetables, forty-two herbs, and twenty-one fruits.

On a sunny May morning, as Peter thinned the carrots and Eileen did the washing, Dorothy Maclean was contacted by a being who was to completely revolutionize the gardens at Findhorn, transforming them from the ordinary to the fantastic. This being was a **Pea Deva**.

Dorothy and the Devas

Today there is a wide measure of agreement, which on the physical side of science approaches almost to unanimity, that the stream of knowledge is heading towards a nonmechanical reality; the universe begins to look more like a great thought than like a great machine. Mind no longer appears as an accidental intruder into the realm of matter; we are beginning to suspect that we ought rather to hail it as the creator and governor of the realm of matter. . . .

—Sir James Jeans (physicist)

Dorothy perceives Devas as thoughts, aspects of growth and creation temporarily forgotten and neglected by modern man. Creation is thought—a vibration, an idea, a seed point. From the divine potential every thought which creates the universe springs forth, and these thoughts are creating it still. Dorothy would ask: From whence sprang the thought of a bit of moss or a larch? Is there anyone who can answer that question with confidence and surety? What carries the archetypal mold of life through space and time to the point where it unfolds into life on a crystal blue planet? Through eons of time the divine potential has differentiated itself again and again into myriad forms and patterns. These thoughts have an energy and potential which is vibrant and the very essence of that which we call life. Of cypress, watercress, and cornflowers there is a thought—a thought which has existed from time immemorial—which permeates the whole of the universe with an identity of its own, unique yet in perfect harmony with all other thoughts. Shall we call these Devas? A Deva is a pattern of life seeking fulfillment—it is everywhere, it cannot die, it simply is.

Dorothy Maclean's life became indirectly intertwined with the Caddys' in 1940 when she accepted an offer by British Intelligence to serve overseas in secretarial capacities at various embassies. She was chaperoned by her new employer from Toronto to New York in the personage of one Sheena Govan, who would ultimately become her spiritual mentor and guide. Her work took her around the world to Panama, Argentina, and Scandinavia, during which time she sought out the mental, meditative, and physical techniques of Sufism from a teacher in Rio de Janeiro. At the end of the war, she quit her job and enrolled in a London art school, eventually meeting Peter and Eileen through her former chaperone, Sheena Govan, now a recognized spiritual teacher.

Sheena Govan was a being whom I could love, respect, and listen to. She sensed a pattern and plan for world growth and trained us for a role in that. Her application of spiritual principles to our private lives went beyond my beloved Sufi teachings. The truth and love she wielded made me ask if I was willing to see the truth, to change and become a true server of God.

Dorothy was working during the day as a Fleet Street secretary and living alone in a flat. One evening, while puttering quietly about, she heard a voice say, "Listen, listen, write it down." She tried to pay no attention to it, thinking in fact that it was a sign that her mind was wandering, but the voice was persistent and began to occur daily. Half wondering if she hadn't better stop meditating altogether, she hesitantly began to write the words down. From that point, a flood of words began to flow through her, but the doubting of her conscious mind censored much of it and just left what she thought to be "jolly well correct."

One day, while visiting Sheena, she discussed these experiences, whereupon Sheena insisted on seeing the "messages." After carefully reading and scrutinizing each one, she told Dorothy that she ought not have so little faith, for what was being transmitted to Dorothy was true and good. She encouraged Dorothy to write everything down, no matter how silly it might sound, and Dorothy began a pattern in her life very similar to Eileen's. Those twenty scribbled notes were a crossroads in her life, for although her mind was saying: "Oh, no, I am not going to get into THAT," she kept on receiving and recording these messages, not with complete trust but with a knowing that this was her path to follow.

Dorothy, an attractive and wizardlike secretary who had perfect credentials and a plush, well-paid job, found that when she moved into this new direction, her friends drew back, not knowing what had come over poor "Dottie," eventually turning their backs on her as a "crank."

She experienced the plight of all twentieth-century mystics surrounded by a church which prefers to see God as a distant Old Testament Jehovah, a church which did not look kindly on people communing with God. Dorothy was dismissed as a "crackpot," and indeed she was, for she had broken the mental shell which maintains selfhood and identity separate from God, becoming instead responsive to a note sounded within her soul resonant to the wholeness and oneness which she called the God within.

From these experiences, it soon became obvious that her life's work was not in London as a secretary. Sheena suggested that she go into service, become a house servant, and that in so doing, she would see and realize different aspects of life. And so she let go of her plush job, good income, flat, and all of her belongings. Her first job was second kitchenmaid in an old people's home. She immediately did some very unkitchenmaidlike things, including spiritual counseling and redecorating at her expense on one of the patient's rooms. She moved on from there to other jobs, bringing her into contact with social strata that had been occluded by her upper-middle-class upbringing. The initial doubts and worries about daily necessities dropped away as she learned that she could live with no money through faith. The new skills, friends, and experiences received in these years of drifting were more than she had known in her entire life until then.

The guidance was useless unless practical to everyday life. That was stressed again and again by Sheena until we were tired of hearing it. But again it would be repeated. Life tested me, swept me out of well-paid jobs into a strange world where God and intuition were the guides, and where the overwhelming lessons of a moneyless, homeless, possessionless, and rootless life were learned. Peter, Eileen, and I all finally ended up in a hotel where we remained for five years, running it according to the spiritual principles we had learned. The hotel was a very specific lead to Findhorn, which was only four miles away. Hotel life was a training in group living, in handling people and looking after visitors, in overcoming inadequacies and in learning about life. Findhorn to us was only a village where we took the boys to swim or to build sand castles; the caravan park was an ugliness that we were thankful to have nothing to do with.

But after six years of dedicated hotel work, to our astonishment we were fired. Where to go, with four hours' notice, all our belongings and the three young boys? We went to the caravan at Findhorn as a temporary measure until our strange destiny returned to normal, as we were sure it would. But destiny did not revoke its conditions, and we stayed on at that caravan park, vainly looking for jobs and muttering to ourselves. We made the best of no job; we continued our spiritual work, living like hermits, and started a garden to help our diet, for "dole" money was not extensive.

When Peter and Eileen first settled into the Hollow, Dorothy moved into the servants' quarters at a village hotel a mile and a half away. Later, when the annex was built on the caravan, she joined them, helping Peter paint and patch things around the caravan or minding the children with Eileen. At night, they would sit around the coal fire and meditate and talk. For Dorothy, it was a waiting time, an interlude which would soon bring on new life patterns. She never expected that she was to stay there for ten years.

From springtime on, Dorothy worked in the garden from early morning until dark, picking stones from the soil or spreading seaweed. She would remain outside all day, being Peter's "donkey," stopping only to eat lunch on the patio at noon. It was a happy time for everyone as the energies that had accumulated during a winter in the caravan were finally being released in their vigorous labors. In the garden the results of their toil were good but not particularly unique, and they were encountering more and more problems in terms of insects and disease.

Then, on May 8, Dorothy sat down to meditate and received the following words: *To those who have an insight into life everything has meaning. For example, there is meaning behind the constant blowing of the wind, a spiritual meaning, in spite of any unpleasant results it brings about. To those whose eyes are open, everything fits into place.*

The forces of nature are something to be felt into, to be stretched out to. . . . One of the jobs for you is to feel into the Nature forces such as the wind, feel its essence and purpose for Me, and be positive and harmonize with that essence. It will not be as difficult as you immediately imagine, because the beings of these forces . . . will be glad to feel a friendly power. All forces are to be felt into, even the sun, the moon, the sea, the trees, the very grass. All are part of My life. All is One life. Play your part in making life one again, with My help.

Dorothy did not know what to make of it. She took this suggestion as a delightful excuse to go for walks or to lie in the sun, but when she shared it with Peter, he saw immediately a way in which she could help the building of the garden. He insisted that Dorothy seek out more information, and the next day she received: *You are to cooperate in the garden by thinking about the Nature Spirits, the higher Nature Spirits, the Spirits of different physical forms, such as the spirits of the clouds, of rain, of the separate vegetables. In the new world their realm will be quite open to humans—or, I should say, humans will be open to them. Be open and seek into the glorious realms of Nature with sympathy and understanding, knowing these beings are of the Light, willing to help but suspicious of human beings.*

These were rather incredible instructions, and Dorothy put off any contact for quite a while. Peter, being practical and highly concerned about the growth of the garden, was badgering her to get on with it; he wanted specifics; he wanted to know why the lettuce was dying and what he could do about bugs. She wondered and hesitated, but as with Eileen, it was Peter who had absolute faith and positively supported the messages. It was his constant pushing along with Dorothy's curiosity that finally prompted her to seek further contact. Thinking it best to start on a rather low and practical level before tackling the rain or the moon, she chose a pea, since peas were growing in the garden and were her favorite vegetable. In the caravan during morning meditation she reached a totally new state of consciousness, and as soon as she gave thought to a Nature Spirit, the Spirit of the Peas, an immediate response was received that was startling in its lucidity and rapidity:

I can speak to you, human. I am entirely directed by my work, which is set out and molded and which I merely bring to fruition. You have come to my awareness. My work is clear before me; the force fields are there to be brought into manifestation regardless of obstacles, and there are many obstacles on this manifested world. You think that slugs, for example, are a greater menace to me than man, but this is not so; slugs are part of the order of things, and the vegetable kingdom holds no grudge against those it feeds. But man takes what he can as a matter of course, giving no thanks, which makes us strangely hostile. Humans generally seem to know not where they are going or why. If they did, what a powerhouse they would be. If they were on the straight course of what is to be done, we could co-operate with them. I have put across my meaning and bid you farewell.

That was the message. Dorothy was stunned. How oddly cogent and direct this being was, whatever it was. And what was it indeed? A spirit? An angel? A being? What do you call it? Certainly not a pea. It was something that seemed to move through and around the materiality that was a garden pea. Dorothy excitedly ran outside to find Peter. She had done it with Peter's encouragement, and she wanted to share it with him. Peter was delighted and equally excited.

The garden was a necessary tool for survival; they needed food in order to live and particularly food with great vitality, as their bodies were definitely changing. But now, through Dorothy, another aspect was being unlocked. The archetypal being that overlighted the form and growth of a plant species had been contacted. Peter did not doubt for a moment that there was a special purpose to this. Great areas of thought and knowledge seemed to be thrown open, to be sought after in additional contacts.

Behind Dorothy's contacts was a deeply rooted feeling: she saw everything as alive. Dorothy read books which related the growth and life of the plant world not only to the quicker forces of season and soil but also to the more subtle and cosmic influences of the moon, planets, and stars. Dorothy had learned to look at the Earth as a living sentient organism and at planets as living beings. Between these living beings, forces were sent out and received.

On May 29 she received: *You are a life force moving about other life forces. As you recognize this and open up to these other forces, you draw near to them and become more and more one with them, and work with them in My purpose. You are receding from the self-centered world that you have created for yourselves and are entering vast new worlds where life is one because it all works together for My good. In the past you have drifted along unconscious of My life. Now seek it, become aware of it, and work with it.*

With Peter's constant prodding and questioning, and Dorothy's attunement to this higher consciousness of Nature, they began to gather a vast store of information on which they based their decisions. Dorothy was told through the Landscape Angel, a being which overlighted the whole geographical area, that wonders could be worked if man entered into a new dimension of cooperation and harmony with the spirits overlighting the garden. Exact instructions were given to Dorothy by the Landscape Angel about preparing the soil, the compost, the watering, the plants, and how to apply liquid manure.

Although I had begun this experiment with a large measure of skepticism, no doubt influenced by limited conceptions of such beings as fairies, as the contact continued and proved valid in giving help with the growth of the garden I accepted the reality of such beings, and we followed out their instructions. This seemed to delight them, particularly our putting into action what they suggested. At first some of them felt very distant and rather unfriendly, which they said was due to the treatment man had given Nature through his greed, thoughtlessness, and misuse. But as they found us heeding what they said, they became more and more helpful and friendly and asked us to plant as many varieties of vegetables as possible.

At least once a day Dorothy initiated a contact which would give precise directions. Peter as well received very strong inner promptings and would ask Dorothy to check and verify his intuitive feelings about the garden, since many of the techniques were directly in conflict with orthodox gardening practices. They followed the instructions given through Dorothy to the letter. *You have overdone the watering, so cut down just a little. It need not be a nightly routine in this climate where the sun is not a daily routine. It is right to have the plants close together, because everything is intensified in the garden. We are pleased at the way the garden is being tackled. We wish you could see the forces now working in the garden: those from below are gradually being drawn up, and ours are coming in great swift waves. No, it is not necessary to put the peat in the garden . . . better in the compost . . . we are speeding up the compost . . . mix.*

Dorothy began to use the word "Deva" (a Hindu word meaning "a being of light") to describe the beings she was contacting.

As they moved into summer hundreds of messages were received from the Devas and other overlighting angels, including:

Dwarf Bean Deva: *The first lot was sown too deeply and before the forces in the garden were great enough. They won't come up properly.*

Tomato Deva: *It is shivery for them, but we shall try to protect. You can give them liquid manure now. Leave the windbreaks on at the moment until the fruit is somewhat formed.*

Spinach Deva: *If you want strong natural growth of the leaf, the plants will have to be wider apart than they are at the moment. By leaving them as they are, you will get overall as much bulk in the leaves, perhaps a little tender, but with not as strong a life force.*

Landscape Angel: *Do not have the idea that a sodden day like today is not good. We can use it for sending down certain forces in the raindrops. All weathers are our métiers in some form or other. As we find a certain condition, we take what benefit we can from it. This seems the obvious thing to do, but we do notice that humans rarely work this way now.*

The sooner you turn the compost, the sooner it will be ready. We should like some sunshine, but the plants are coming along well. It is good for any of you to come and admire us—it adds to our well-being.

Marrow Deva: *We are glad of the direct contact! We feel and see the forces in the garden, but the contact is also a delight—it is a novelty. At the moment we do not need a lot of extra water. The plants are progressing well, are happy and well adjusted.*

As each new plant was introduced into the garden by Peter, Dorothy would welcome it and contact the individual Deva of the species. When questions of a general nature arose, these would be answered by the Landscape Angel, a spokesman for all the Devas, who told them that it was vitally important to think about the garden and plants in terms of radiations instead of separate aspects such as chemicals and elements. All the gardeners were told that the most important thing they could do was to radiate from within a sense of love and appreciation to the plants and that in this way every single person there could participate in the creation of the garden.

Peter's radiations are forceful and purposeful, and these qualities can be used by us to add to the plant growth. Every gardener contributes to his garden in this way unconsciously, but those who are consciously aligned can contribute much more. Certain people can stimulate plant growth, while some have a depressing effect and would draw from the plant forces themselves. Happiness has an especially good effect on plants, and children playing does as well. Our radiations are interwoven much more than you realize, for whereas the nature spirits shy away from human beings, they cannot help but be affected by their vibrations, for they are open creatures without the many skins that humans have.

Toward the latter part of June, people were beginning to come to see the garden, and after seeing it they told their friends about it. A steady stream of visitors began to pour in to see the amazing growth, greenness, and abundance which was being produced in the sandy patch. The garden was becoming a local showplace, and people who came found it hard to believe that the first seed had been sown just a few months previously. The Scots, famous for being good gardeners, would come and look about and just shake their heads, unable to make it out. Although the plants at first were susceptible to insects and apt to wilt, they built up resistance as the life forces in the soil were built up. Just across the way in the caravan site, another garden had been planted at the same time. There the Brussels sprouts had grown two or three inches and then stopped, whereas Peter's were already two feet high.

At midsummer, when the days were twenty hours long and the sunsets lingered on the horizon for hours, Dorothy and the Caddys spent most of the daylight hours outside. After their daily swim in the ocean, they made lunches of large salads consisting entirely of produce from the garden. Glowing and abundant health descended upon them all.

In June, Peter started on the final piece of garden for that year, which completed a circle around their caravan. To the dead sand and soil were added cummings, peat, compost, soot, and lime; a fence was built to keep the rabbits out. Although Peter and Dorothy were working very closely now, Dorothy still felt reluctant to ask down-to-earth and practical questions of the Devas, for she felt in some ways that this might be "beneath them." But Peter continued to insist on the practical, and the results kept coming in. Soon even local farmers were coming to the Caddys to buy vegetables, and people in town who heard about it would drive out on weekends to buy the surplus produce.

At first the Deva messages were mostly of a practical nature, concentrating on those aspects of the garden which were of timely importance, but as summer moved on, the messages broadened out and the Devas revealed themselves more clearly to Dorothy. It became apparent that what was coming through was not a spirit attached to one particular pea plant or tomato bush but rather a spirit which was the plan, the mold, and architect of all peas on the earth.

Physicists, after seeking the essence of the material world, have hypothesized that all energy is a thought, and according to Dorothy, the Devas are archetypal thoughts or energies.

Physics sees matter as energy, a momentary illusion in a universe which knows no permanence; it sees a world which has no bounds, no divisions, and fewer and fewer rules and laws. In this world, physics and the I Ching have much in common, for both seek to understand the phenomenology of change. Once realizing the fundamental illusion of matter, one either perceives the universe with reverence or, like the physicist who shot himself when he discovered his chair didn't exist, one goes mad.

The new scientific paradigm is a bright blossom in a world dominated by the technology of the old, a science which treated life as mechanical, where living organisms responded to fixed laws which man discovered and applied. Nowhere has this been more true than in the world of plants. We have studied, dissected, experimented, and examined the whole world of plants and have developed sciences which make plants our servants. Unwillingness in the plant world to completely cooperate has always been met with new technologies, new ways to assert dominance over a life form which we approached as one to subjugate and control. The vast power and resources unlocked in the two world wars have been turned over to "peaceful" pursuits, not the least of which was soil technology. The discovery of the NPK principle in plant growth heralded an age of facile, simplistic thinking which has set us on a collision course with destruction. We admittedly knew very little about plants and soil before the 1860s, but in that ignorance was a certain respect for nature, for in not knowing what we were doing, we simply imitated nature around us. We have farmed some areas of the world for thousands of years. The rule was simply take what you need and give everything else back. Sir Albert Howard founded organic agriculture because of a vision he had in a forest, seeing the rich layers of humus constantly replenished by the waste of trees growing from it. Most farmers until the Industrial Revolution did the same. When chemicals were introduced and yields climbed appreciably, it was only the exceptional farmer who knew one could not bypass laws of nature. Yes, yields could be raised, altered, and forced, but we would have to pay for it eventually.

We learned to make hybrids that could grow bigger and faster than their parent stock. The size, shape, and even color of plants was altered by methodically applying all our knowledge of genetic manipulation. We could even grow square tomatoes that could be machine picked and compactly shipped. It was all a "miracle," and the fact that the tomatoes tasted pretty much like the cardboard they were wrapped in seemed somehow to be lost in all the hoopla and self-congratulatory publicity.

Our food, in less than a century, has been transformed, and it was only because of the insularity of the urban environment that people forgot what food was and what it tasted like. At first mothers knew they had to peel this new food in order to eliminate the sprays, but then they even forgot that. Factory farming has reduced the quality and flavor of food to a shadow of its original perfection. The chemical food industry has grown not so much out of its successes but out of necessity to cover its tracks. We are left with the twentieth-century tomato, a tomato which does not look like a tomato, which does not taste like a tomato, which is dependent upon frequent applications of poison to protect it from its environment, which is nurtured in greenhouses where there is no soil, only a thin, amber, ill-smelling liquid which supplies "everything it needs."

If we wish to reduce the world to simplistic mechanical laws governing so many chemicals, atoms, and molecules, then we must be prepared to live with the results. Is the result going to be life without life? Are our life sciences truly living? Is there anywhere on the planet to study what life is? Or has every department, every specialist branch of science, in its rush to approach the core become dim and blind? Has Dorothy stumbled across something that has been atrophied from the consciousness of human beings? Have we lost, in our blind pursuit of truth and wisdom, every faculty that would grant that which we seek? The axiom "you become what you hate" is never more apparent than today. We have tried to banish from the planet the darkness and ignorance of the ages. We have heralded a new age of discovery and civilization for mankind. We have been blowing the horn of the golden age while reviling the dark superstition of the past, the abysmal obscurant patterns of thought which prevented us from seeing the world as it "really is." One cannot help but wonder if we have not instead embodied a greater ignorance and folly which beggars all that has preceded it, bringing a total lack of understanding that has created a howling apocalyptic nightmare with which the planetary body must now wrestle in order to survive. We are told that the pollution and destruction caused by technology will be solved by technology, that we need more power to clean up what the generation of power has created, an argument so absurd that it merits no response. It is the rank breath of a monstrous force which feeds upon itself and breeds contemptuously. In a world of such utter chaos and lack of direction, the message of the Devas takes on a certain prophetic truth: *As the rain falls on the just and unjust, we help to produce food for the good and the evil; the moral side of things is not our concern. We merely follow our destinies. We are man's friend or enemy depending on man himself. Our life is for the good; but man is making mincemeat of all life forces. On this level we are stable and man does not affect us, but further down where he is, he can, and he has, and we cannot answer for the consequences. Shall we not co-operate and build a new relationship?*

From talks with Dorothy and after close examination of hundreds of pages of messages received over the years from the Devas, there emerges a pattern and logic which describes a level of existence hinted at by cultures throughout history. Dorothy felt that through the contact with the Devas a bridge had been built to a level of existence and consciousness which had been submerged and buried. It was her desire to stay as close as possible to that contact and to see fulfilled within the garden every instruction and message given.

The Devic world emphasized that man has to do one thing in order to reverse the trend of events on the planet: he has to recognize within himself the Divinity and wholeness of which he is a part. He must touch that core which perceives itself as a part of all things, all beings, and all aspects of creation. In that recognition and touching the distinction between the outer and inner is erased and vanishes.

To us the question of a Nature which "talks" is a rather uncomfortable one. For Peter and Dorothy there could be no question. No further proof was necessary. Every instruction received turned out to be exactly right for the garden, and the garden itself was resplendent and magnificent. Perhaps communication with plants isn't quite so far out as we imagine. The rash of research and literature into the field of plant communication has demonstrated rather startling results. Most of this research has concentrated on whether Nature can hear us. But the real question might be whether we can hear nature, and after talking with Dorothy, the answer may be yes. The lack of contact between humans and Nature is a recent phenomenon, the exception rather than the rule, for human beings have been in communication with nature spirits, the Devas, the spirit of forests and stars, since the dawn of history.

The earth, once white and molten, represents a thought. It was a fire in the heavens, glowing as a sun, visited by the Deva of the Wind which came and blew across the surface, playing with the Fire Deva until all was mediated. The Deva of Water and Rain formed and collected in the skies and fell to earth. Great clouds of steam issued forth from the surface, the skies were enlivened and heavy with its presence, and across the surface the Wind Deva began to cool, carve, and chisel away at the crust of the planet. It created pools and eddies, lakes and streams, and bigger bodies which we know as oceans. With each successive change, a new Deva or impulse came forth until, like a procession, did the Earth receive the new hosts, each Deva bringing with it a variation of life ever present in the divine potential. The Earth prepared itself to receive and serve the thought of a man and a woman. The Earth would be their temple and guardian; the heavens would be their guide and vision. Humans affirmed the link between the infinite spirit and the totality of matter. They related from the highest spiritual planes to the most concrete levels of form. The Earth was for humanity to enshrine, to make holy, to blend their unique qualities and work as a family in cooperation with the Devas, the spiritual stewards of the planet.

Are the millions of ways that nature is interlinked mere evolutionary compromise? Is it a coincidence that the wind rustles and blows the autumn leaves to the ground, where they rot and feed the roots of new growth? Is there not within the snow on the ground the water which shall nourish the spring grass and saplings on which the deer shall break their winter fast? Everything in nature is co-operation. The water rises up from the sea to the loftiest peaks, is purified in the highest reaches of the atmosphere, and then it drops, clear and diamond-perfect like tiny jewels, to a thirsty earth to move again with ease to the sea. Cycles work in perfect harmony. Within this is there not our lost pattern and a forgotten teaching?

We, as overseeing causative forces of manifestation, would share with you a little of our consciousness. Everything manifest is in our care, and we know its state, for under God we make plain His creation. All is in our consciousness. Consciousness is an open book for all to share with us, for we are so much one that what we know is not separate from what our neighbor knows.

How can we wholly express the light and loving intention of all creation, the sparkling dynamic purpose of perfection which is the motive of all that is, some little part of which goes through our hands? How can we tell you how we dance with joy, that the sun dances and the moon dances and we dance around them and in them? The earth itself dances at heart and is beginning to dance at more than heart as man rises up out of limitation and turns his eyes back toward reality.

In all this we are absolutely and utterly free. There is no freedom unless one is completely part of all; until then freedom is limited. For all are one, and if any believe other-wise, they are circumscribing their part in the whole and imprisoning themselves in the part.

You may have a garden in your care, and on looking into it one day you find that something has happened, that un-known to you certain growth has been made—but we know all at once and nothing is closed to us. Our consciousness is a dipping into a sea of knowing, for all forces are connected, and it is as if a loving computer links all because all can-not otherwise be. . . . You have to be whole to see the whole; until then, parts have to be seen separately. We see wholly with regard to our work.

And we would say to you with one voice that our focused attention is on mankind and that it is clearer than in the recent past and more precise in definition because you are beginning to respond and be aware of our activities. At this we rejoice and are glad, for the connections between us are greater than you realize, and it seems strange to us that you should be unconscious of so much of your own being. We see you like icebergs with seven-eighths of your consciousness submerged and only one-eighth alive. We retain the consciousness with which we have been gifted and thus can plainly see our part. We are in the line of consciousness from the One Great Whole to the smallest unit of life, and therefore we perform the miracles which you see in the growth of the seed.

We are forever one with you in spirit.

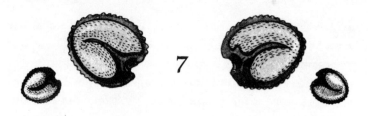
The Piper on the Mound

O see ye not yon narrow road
  So thick beset wi' thorns and briers?
That is the path of Righteousness,
  Though after it but few inquires.

And see ye not yon braid, braid road
  That lies across the lily leven?
That is the path of Wickedness,
  Though some call it the Road to Heaven.

And see ye not yon bonny road
  That winds about yon fernie brae?
That is the road to fair Elfland,
  Where thou and I this night maun gae.

Peter Caddy was the embodiment of Man in the garden representing man's search for ordering the wildness of nature. Peter's role became one of structuring and organizing, of previsualizing the possibilities, seeing that perfection was the goal, and profusion the result.

It was Dorothy who in her contact with the Devic world gave Peter tools he never imagined. It was her link that provided the insight into life processes and consciousness that enabled the phenomenal to emerge from the sand. The Devic world seemed at once to encourage and enforce all of Man's energies and ideas while refusing to get too involved with Man. There was an aloofness innate in the Devas which gave Peter plenty of elbow room. There was an equanimity and acceptance which gave man great latitude for errors and understanding for faults. The Devas even apologized when an apricot couldn't take the cold and finally died.

But in 1966 a third force entered the garden which was to create a triangular relationship, further enhancing the tremendous growth and profusion of life while providing counterpoint to Man's desires. This was the world of the Nature Spirits overlighted by the god Pan. And it was discovered by the bright flickering eyes of one Robert Ogilvie Crombie, sometimes known as Roc.

Crombie has lived in a 150-year-old drawing room flat in Edinburgh since his twenties. At seventy-five, he still spryly negotiates the three flights of stairs up to the flat. Crombie has never actually lived at Findhorn, but his contact with the Nature Spirits solidified a casual relationship he had with Peter Caddy, bringing him into a deeper partnership and cooperation with Dorothy and Eileen and the development of the community and garden.

His flat is crammed with seven thousand books which he has found of particular interest over his lifetime. A congenital heart defect discovered during the last three weeks of exams at Edinburgh University forced him to drop out and miss his degree. The enforced sedentary existence turned him into an even more avid student. Schooling never stopped; the restrictions on the physical stimulated the mental movement further, and he moved into photography, electronics, music (the piano), and continued his training in chemistry, physics, and mathematics.

His early scientific pursuits have grounded him into an objective search for truth. He has always sought experiential confirmation for his thoughts and ideas as well as his experiments. Yet, the fifty years of study have not turned him into the stuffed owl on the antiquarian's bookshelf. Only last year, he received a stereo and the complete works of Karlheinz Stockhausen through the composer's wife because of his understanding and interest in contemporary music which he demonstrates in talks and lectures.

But whereas his background seems "normal" enough and certainly not unusual in any obvious way, there is about Crombie an air of mystery, the mystery one feels when seeing a long-forgotten object from the past. The memory races through the mental stacks, but the book is gone. Who is he? Don't I know him? The only knowing allowed is the knowing that you knew, and every moment is pregnant with the expectation that Roc will say something that will reveal the common touchstone. It is a musky afternoon in early summer. A figure of a man ambles through the hazy warmth, sees you, and stops, reflects, looks again, and then wanders off with a glint of recognition in his eyes.

Or you are transported to one of those paintings in the British Museum showing a burnished brass globe with misshapen continents while strewn about a carven table are rolls of yellowed parchment revealing hints of Pythagorean tracings; in the corner, a white bearded man mumbles to himself as he squints in the dim light of a beeswax candle at Ptolemy's Almagest.

Ogilvie is the palingenesis of an Elizabethan scholar, highly dignified, stately and precise, delighting the Queen with his humor while counseling her to be aware of the transiting of Saturn in her seventh house. Ancestral barriers seem to rise and fall about Roc like playful mists. He is at once warm, friendly, and generous to all about him and at the same time completely inscrutable, an enigma beyond history and culture, sitting in front of you in a large overstuffed chair, dwarfed yet strangely larger than life, his outer suit crumpled up about his woolen pullover, his eyes flicking about the room like a lizard's tongue.

Sometimes people are unnerved by the absolute stillness of his outer visage and the absence of what we think of as personality. There is indeed a charm, an utterly beguiling manner and expression which is disarming in its innocence and captivating in its openness, but it is the innocence of the ancients, not of youth. When he speaks to you he is wandering in areas of his mind which you don't have a hint of. If Merlin's owl alighted on his shoulder, you would hardly be surprised. He seems enwrapped in an amniotic fluid of a world myth which threatens to break any moment; he is a chrysalis neatly hanging from the old modern reality.

I felt in him a depth of patience which alludes to a soul quietly waiting for man to awaken from a prolonged slumber. It is as if there has been a spell cast upon mankind, and Crombie waits and watches while it wears off and the sands of sleep fall from our eyes. He seems to be far off in some recess of inner space from whence he glances back and wonders: "Are you coming?"

He speaks of his experiences in Scottish lilt, clearly and directly with a voice that resonates from a large frame. It is the voice of reasoned and well-thought-out phrases, often eloquent, pausing in order to be accurate and not misspeak. When he speaks of the spirits of the Nature Kingdom, it is not with a subtle indifference that eight years of contact could breed, but it is with awe and wonder.

When he speaks he sits quite contentedly, hands neatly folded in his lap, eyes alight with the fondness a Scotsman knows in telling a good story. There is humor, a relaxed laugh, and an easy dignity. It is a story he tells well.

In major cities there are great parks in which older people slowly walk about or sit on benches looking rather contentedly at their surroundings. If you were to walk into Edinburgh Royal Botanic Garden, you would see them scattered about the park amid ancient trees, holly bushes, and random wooden benches. In March of 1966, Ogilvie

Crombie, taking his favorite stroll, had just left the heath gardens.

"It was a beautiful afternoon, warm and sunny. I had left the path and crossed an expanse of grass to the bottom of a slope. There was a wooden seat just in front of a large beech tree, and I sat down on it. It was very close to the tree, so that I was leaning my shoulders and the back of my head against the trunk. I always feel very much at peace in the Garden, but on this particular day I was feeling very alert, very wide awake.

"I have always had a great love for trees and a sense of affinity with them, in spite of being mainly a town dweller. I became, in some way, identified with this tree—aware of the movement of the sap in the trunk and even of the infinitely slow growth of the roots. There was a decided heightening of awareness and a tremendous sense of exhilaration. I had the odd feeling that something was going to happen. I felt fully awake and full of energy.

"I was sitting in the light of the afternoon sun. The crocuses were just beginning to come out. The garden wasn't crowded that day at all. There were a few people walking along the paths, but I was off the path down a slope. On the whole, I was quite alone there.

"This heightened awareness continued to grow, and there was an extraordinary feeling that something was about to happen. I looked at the grass and then the trees, and then the bark of the trees. It was all intensely beautiful. I wasn't thinking about anything, but I knew something was happening—there was the fullest experiencing of being very much alive. I was awake and excited in some new way.

"And then suddenly it happened.

"I saw something moving from the corner of my eye, something that distracted me. I looked and saw a figure dancing around a tree some twenty-five yards away. And then I looked again. It was quite startling. It was a beautiful figure about three feet tall. I thought: 'Something's happened. I must be going mad. I can't believe *this*!' I pinched myself and said, 'Yes, I know who I am, where I live,' things like that. I wasn't dreaming, but who is *that*? He must be mad!

"I looked at the other people. I looked back at him. He seemed just as solid. The boy is made up, I thought. He could not be—there was something about him that was not human. Although he was moving, I could see shaggy legs and cloven hooves, pointed chin and ears, and the two little horns on his forehead. I watched in utter disbelief, not trusting my own eyes. In spite of feeling so wide awake, I thought I must have fallen asleep.

"He came closer to another tree, and I could see the brown hair on his head and legs. His eyes seemed brown and dark, and his skin was a light honey color, very much like the color of the trees. He was naked, but his legs were covered with fine hair. If he were a real boy, I would have said he was ten or eleven years old. But he was not a real boy.

"There was something about him that was not human. He was a strange creature, the like of which I had never seen before. An hallucination? There were one or two other people walking about in the Garden. I looked at them and then back at this beautiful little being. He was still there and seemed as solid and real as they were. I tried then to explain this thing and rationalize it. But suddenly something brought me up sharply: What was I trying to do? Here was a strange and wonderful experience. Incredible, yes, but why should I not accept it, see what happens, and sort it out later? I stopped trying to analyze it and watched the little being with delight.

"He danced around the tree, moving his arms about, prancing around the trunk several times. He seemed balanced on his hooves as he pirouetted over to another tree. He circled it three times and then came dancing over the center of the grass and sat opposite a couple who were seated at a bench. He examined them curiously for some time, intently interested in their every movement and action. He then leaped up from the grass and came dancing over to where I was sitting. He stood looking at me for a moment and then sat cross-legged in front of me. He put his chin in his hands and cocked his head slightly. I looked at him. He was very real. No doubt about that, but I wasn't sure that I was seeing him with my physical eyes, though when I closed them he was not there. I bent forward and said: 'Hallo.'

"He leaped to his feet as if he had been startled out of his wits. He took a few steps back and then cautiously approached again. He stared at me.

" 'Can you see me?' he asked.

" 'Yes.'

" 'I don't believe it. Humans can't see us.'

" 'Oh?'

" 'What am I like?'

"I described him as I saw him. Still looking bewildered and unsure of himself, he began to dance in small circles.

" 'What am I doing?'

"I told him. He stopped dancing and said: 'You must be seeing me.' He danced across to the seat beside me, sat down, and turned toward me. He looked up and said, 'Why are human beings so stupid?'

" 'In what way stupid?' I replied.

"What were the strange coverings they had, some of which could be taken off? Why did they not go about in their natural state as he did?

"I told him that the skins were called clothes and that we wear them for protection and for warmth, and because it was not considered right to be without them.

" 'Why do you go dashing about in boxes on wheels sometimes bumping into each other? Is it a game?'

"He told me he lived in the Garden, and that his work

was to help the growth of the trees. He went on to say that the Nature Spirits had lost interest in humans, since they have been made to feel that they are neither believed in nor wanted. He thought that men were foolish to think that they could do without the Nature Spirits.

"I told him some people did believe in them and wanted their help. There was a wonderful sense of companionship with this being. I felt an amazing harmony with him sitting beside me. A communication was taking place between us that did not need to be put into words. We sat there for some time in silence, and finally I noticed that it was time to go home. I rose to leave.

"He told me to call him when I returned and that he would come.

"I asked him his name. He said it was Kurmos.

" 'Could you come and visit me?' I asked.

" 'Yes, if you invite me.'

" 'I do. I shall be delighted if you will come and visit me.'

" 'You do believe in me?'

" 'Yes, of course I do. I have much affection for the Nature Spirits.' This was true, although he was the first one I had actually seen.

" 'Then I'll come now.'

"We walked to the west gate of the gardens, out into Arboretum Road and through the streets of Edinburgh to my home. I was amused to have him walking beside me, wondering what the reaction would be from passers-by if he were visible to them as he was to me.

"We entered my flat, and Kurmos went running over to the bookshelves. He looked at them for some time with great interest.

" 'What are these, and . . . why do you have so many?'

"I explained to him that they contained facts, ideas, speculations, and theories, accounts of past events, stories invented by writers and so on, all of which were written down, put into print, and made up into books which could be read by others. I do not know how much of this he understood. He looked rather puzzled.

" 'Why? You can get all the knowledge you want by simply wanting it.'

"It was my turn to look puzzled. I replied that human beings could not do that. We had to be content to get our knowledge or facts from other people, or from books.

"Again, from time to time we sat in silence and a contented harmony. Then he got up, for it was time for him to return to the Gardens. The door of the room was open, and he walked out into the hall. I followed him, and because he looked so solid and real, I opened the door onto the landing. He passed me and ran lightly down the stairs. As he reached the bottom step, he faded out.

"And after he had gone, the impact of the experience began to sink in. I wondered if I had been in the Garden at all, or if I'd fallen asleep and dreamed the whole thing. It was an astonishing experience, one which I am certain I could not have imagined. My imagination works on the prosaic and practical levels and is not inclined to fantasy. And why a faun? That puzzled me.

"The next time I went to the Gardens I called to him and he was immediately by my side. I did not want to ask him questions; the wonderful harmony and companionship that I felt from him were enough, though I knew that here was infinite nature wisdom combined with the naïveté of a child. We had several meetings after that.

"In late April, I was leaving a friend's house fairly late at night and had begun to go back to my flat. I had to cross what was known as the Meadows, a very wide green belt on the south side of Edinburgh castle. I had gone through on what is called Meadow walk, down another street to George's Bridge. I could see down Princes Street, Edinburgh's main street with its continuous buildings on the north side only. On the south side at the east end is the North British Hotel; at the west end, St. John's Church;

and halfway along the street the two Greek-style buildings, the Royal Scottish Academy and, immediately behind it, the National Gallery. Opposite Princes Street is the Castle, perched high on its rock with the long ridge leading down to Holyrood, carrying to High Street—and the buildings and street of the Old Town. These are linked to the middle of Princes Street by the Mound, a street running along a built-up mound providing a fine view of the city.

"It was a beautiful evening, and there were few people about as I walked down the Mound. I was thinking how peaceful it was at the moment. And then as I turned the corner into the last part of the street which runs down the side of the National Gallery, I walked into an extraordinary 'atmosphere.'

"I had never before encountered anything like it. It was as if I had no clothes on and was walking through a medium denser than air but not as dense as water. I could feel it against my body. It produced a sensation of warmth and tingling like a mixture of pins and needles in an electric shock. It was so unusual that it is difficult to describe. This was accompanied by the same heightened awareness and feeling of expectation that I had in the Gardens.

"Then I realized that I was not alone. A figure was walking beside me—a figure taller than myself. It was a faun radiating a tremendous sort of power. I glanced up at him. Surely this was not my little friend. We walked on.

" 'Well, aren't you afraid of me?' he boomed out.

"We were still walking, and I thought about his question. I realized that I was not afraid at all, although by every right I ought to have been.

" 'No.'

"He did not hesitate for a moment: 'Why not? All human beings are afraid of me.'

" 'I feel no evil in your presence. I do not feel afraid.' And I wasn't, but nevertheless I could feel this figure looming over me.

" 'Do you know who I am?'

"I did at that moment. It suddenly hit me who this 'faun' was. 'Yes, I know who you are.'

" 'Then you ought to be afraid. Your word 'panic' comes from the fear my presence causes.'

" 'I am not afraid.'

"He seemed to stop his intense questions for a moment and paused. Then he said: 'Can you give me a reason?'

"The answer came to me immediately: 'It may be because of my feeling of affinity with your subjects, the earth spirits and the woodland creatures.'

" 'Do you believe in my subjects?'

" 'Yes.'

" 'Do you love my subjects?'

"I thought for a moment and realized that it was true. Many of my feelings were coming out under this insistent questioning. 'Yes, I do.'

" 'In that case, do you love me?'

" 'Why not?'

" 'DO YOU LOVE ME?'

" 'Yes!'

"He looked at me with a strange smile and a glint in his eyes. He had deep, mysterious brown eyes.

" 'You know, of course, that I am the devil? You have just said that you love the devil.'

" 'No, you are not the devil. You are the god of the woodlands and countryside. There is no evil in you.'

" 'Did not the early church take me as a model for the devil? Look at my cloven hooves, my shaggy legs, and the horns on my forehead.'

" 'The church turned all pagan gods and spirits into devils, fiends, and imps.'

" 'Was the church wrong then?'

" 'The church did it with the best of intentions from its own point of view. But it was wrong. The ancient gods are not necessarily devils.'

"We crossed Princes Street and turned right toward St. David Street. As we turned the corner he said to me: 'What do I smell like?'

"Since he joined me I had been aware of a wonderful scent of pine woods, of damp leaves, of newly turned earth, and of woodland flowers. I told him.

" 'Don't I smell rank like a goat?'

" 'No, you don't. There is a faint, musklike animal smell, like the fur of a healthy cat. It is pleasant—almost like incense. Are you still claiming to be the devil?'

" 'I have to find out what you think of me. It's important.'

" 'Why?'

" 'For a reason.'

" 'Won't you tell me what it is?'

" 'Not now. It will become apparent in time.'

"We walked on and crossed the end of George Street. He was walking very close beside me.

" 'You don't mind me walking beside you,' he said.

" 'Not in the least.'

"He put his arm around my shoulder, and I felt the physical contact. I was very much aware of a physical presence.

" 'You don't mind if I touch you?' he continued.

" 'No.'

" 'You really feel no repulsion or fear?'

" 'None.'

" 'Excellent.'

"I was terribly curious to know why he was making this determined effort to produce a sign of fear. I am not a brave man and have been scared before in my life. There are many things that would scare me out of my life. But, for some reason or other, I felt no fear of this being. Awe, because of his power, but not fear—only love.

"I did not know then that for his purpose he had to find someone who showed no fear of him. He is a great being —the god of the whole elemental kingdom as well as of the animal, vegetable, and mineral kingdoms. People may feel uneasy in his presence because of the awe he inspires, but there ought to be no fear. 'All human beings are afraid of me.' He had not said this as a threat, but with sadness. 'Did not the early Christian Church make me a model for the devil?' That is why he is feared—because of the image projected onto him. This image must be lifted off him so that his nature may be revealed. That is why he had to find someone who did not fear him.

"We turned into Queen Street, and as we passed the post office I asked him where his pipes were. He smiled at the question: 'I do have them, you know.'

"And there he was, holding them between his hands. He began to play a curious melody. I had heard it in woods before, and I have often heard it since, but it is so elusive that so far I have been unable to remember it afterward. When we reached the downstairs main door of the house where I live, he disappeared. I had a strong feeling, however, that he was still with me when I went in.

"The strange encounter made a strong impression on me. I had no idea why it had happened or why this being had chosen to show himself to me. It looked as if the meeting with the little faun in the Botanic Gardens had been a preliminary step in bringing it about. I felt reasonably certain that neither of the beings was imaginary; they were much too real and unusual. It left me wondering what was going to happen next.

"Well, the next meeting was early in May on Iona in the Hermit's Cell, a ring of stones which is all that is left of the cell where Saint Columba used to go in retreat. It is about halfway across the island, almost on a level with the Abbey. I was there with two friends; one of them was Peter. I was standing in the center of the ring, facing in the direction of the Abbey which was hidden from sight by rising ground. In front of me was a gentle grassy slope.

"I became aware of a large figure lying in the ground. I

could see him through the grass. It appeared to be a monk in a brown habit with the hood pulled over the head so that the features were concealed. His feet were toward the cell. As I watched, he raised his hands and rolled back the hood. It was Pan. He rose up out of the ground and stood facing us, an immense figure. He smiled and said: 'I am the servant of Almighty God, and I and my subjects are willing to come to the aid of mankind in spite of the way he has treated us and abused nature, if he affirms belief in us and asks for our help.'

"It became apparent that what was happening was a sort of reconciliation between the Nature Kingdom and man.

"Another encounter took place in September of the same year, 1966, at Attingham Park. I had attended a weekend course conducted by Sir George Trevelyan. Before leaving on the Monday morning, I was prompted to go to an area known as the Mile Walk on the extensive grounds of Attingham. The walk starts at a point on the bank of the River Tern where there are many trees and bushes. I followed it until I came to a slight bend in the river where a huge cedar tree with a seat around it is situated. To the left of the tree, at a right angle to the river, is the beginning of the Rhododendron Walk.

"I sat there for some time enjoying the beauty of the place. After a while I rose and went into the walk. As I did so, I felt a great buildup of power and an increase in awareness to a high degree. Colors and forms became more significant. I was aware of every single leaf on the bushes and trees, of every blade of grass on the path standing out with startling clarity. It was as if physical reality had become even more solid—a strange sharpening of vision. It is an overwhelming experience when it happens and nearly impossible to describe in words. It is a thing one must experience for oneself to understand fully. I had the impression of complete reality, and all that lies within and beyond it felt immediately imminent. The sense of awe and wonder this produced is not easy to convey. There was an acute feeling of being one with nature in a complete way as well as being one with the Divine, which produced great exultation.

"I was aware that he was walking by my side and of a strong bond between us. He stepped behind me and then walked into me so that we became one and I saw the surroundings through his eyes. At the same time, part of me —the recording, observing part—stood aside. The experience was not a form of possession but of identification.

"The moment he stepped into me, the woods became alive with myriads of beings—elementals, nymphs, dryads, fauns, elves, gnomes, fairies—far too numerous to catalogue. They varied in size from tiny little beings a fraction of an inch in height—like the ones I saw swarming about on a clump of toadstools—to beautiful elfin creatures three or four feet tall. Some of them were dancing round me in a ring; all were welcoming and full of rejoicing. The Nature Spirits love and delight in the work they do and have to express this in movement.

"I felt as if I were outside time and space. Everything was happening in the Now. It is impossible to give more than a faint impression of the actuality of this experience, but I would stress the exultation and the feeling of joy and delight. In spite of the intense exhilaration, there was an underlying peace, contentment, and a sense of spiritual presence.

"I found myself in a clearing at the end of this part of the Rhododendron Walk, where there is a great oak tree. I turned and walked back the way I had come. I now had pipes in my hands and was aware of shaggy legs and cloven hooves. I began to dance down the path, playing the pipes —the melody I had heard. The numerous birds responded, their songs making an exquisite counterpoint to the music of the pipes. All the nature beings were active, many dancing as they worked.

"When I had reached the spot where the experience had started, the heightened awareness began to fade and he withdrew, leaving me once more my ordinary self. I stopped dancing and walked on. The pipes had gone. The change from this strange ecstatic experience to the normal reality of everyday life was not a disappointment. What I had experienced was still there; it is always there, as it is part of the true reality. Because of our dulled sense and our habit of going through life wearing materialistic blinders in a condition verging on sleepwalking, we are unaware of the fantastic beauty of the life around us. Of course, it would not do if we were aware of it all the time; it would be too overwhelming and make us incapable of performing our daily tasks. Many of us, however, could well be much more aware of our surroundings without doing that.

"Approaching the end of the path and the cedar tree, I began to walk sedately, which was just as well, since a boy was sitting on the seat under the tree. It might have been disconcerting for at least one of us if I had come dancing down the path playing invisible pipes at my age.

"There have been other significant meetings, of course. I have been aware of him many times since and have also been aware of a variety of Nature Spirits and am able to communicate with them. Because I had responded without fear, he used me as a link. This does not make me important in myself—I am simply a channel he can use, but I feel greatly privileged that this is so and that I have been given the ability to contact these wonderful beings and communicate with them.

"The main reason for this communication was the contribution it made to the work in the Findhorn Garden and its development. By bringing onto a conscious level the already existing links with the Nature Spirits, guidance and knowledge could be received complementary to Dorothy's link with the Devic World. We were establishing contact and cooperation between three kingdoms at Findhorn, the Devas, Nature, and Man. This became the aim of the Garden, and it is now well on its way to realization.

"We may think of the Devas as angelic beings, and it seems that they design the archetypal pattern for each species and channel down the required energies for its manifestation on earth.

"The Nature Spirits, on the other hand, may be regarded as the builders. Working according to the archetypal design, they form and build up what may be called the 'etheric counterpart' or 'body' of the plant from the energies channeled down by the Devas.

"Of course, many people would question the existence of such a thing. Of course, it cannot be scientifically proven at the moment, though no doubt this will be possible in the future. To the scientists the whole plan of the plant is in the seed, contained within the genetic code of the DNA molecule. Plant the seed and the tree will grow, needing no help from such dubious entities as Devas and Nature Spirits. This is a legitimate point of view, and little can be done to change the opinion of those who hold it. It is usually a waste of time to try.

"Most of us know that we are more than just a physical body. According to some, we have an etheric body and even other higher bodies. We are the incarnate spirit. The plants have at least etheric bodies, if not higher ones as well. Is it not possible that molecules such as DNA also have an etheric counterpart? Could it replicate without it? Might there even be an elemental being working with that counterpart? Could the plant really grow without its counterpart and the beings associated with it? I know this is fantastic nonsense to the scientist. I met a professor in Aberdeen, however, who said that the idea of tiny fairy fingers helping to unfold a butterfly's wings and blossoms was not a totally unacceptable idea to him, since science has never really explained satisfactorily what the mechanism is that accomplishes this.

"It is important to know that a plant grows within the etheric counterpart brought into existence by the Nature Spirits. By interfering with the natural growth of a plant in trying to alter the form through artificial means, often using force, man can depart from the archetypal design. Apart from the fear and pain produced in the plant, this can bring about lack of alignment with the counterpart, causing further discomfort and distress to the plant.

"No doubt there are times when man is justified in modifying nature's handiwork if the reasons for doing so are sufficiently strong. But instead of using force it would be better to ask the Nature Spirits to bring it about by modifying the etheric counterpart. As they have the infinite power to do so, they could—and would—do this if they were convinced that it was reasonable and a help to mankind, not simply for expediency. At the moment they are limited in their actions by the general disbelief in their power and even in their existence. I hope this general disbelief will gradually be dispelled as more and more people begin to accept the idea of the existence of elemental beings who are prepared to help man, and so hasten the full cooperation with their kingdom. I can visualize new kinds of horticulture and agriculture being developed as well as harmful methods being discarded.

"It cannot be emphasized enough that the elemental beings and their god, Pan, are servants of God and function according to His will only.

"Many people will find it impossible to believe me. This I understand. It is difficult to comprehend at first the idea of elves, gnomes, and fairies working in the garden. They might feel it is a lot of nonsense. It may be helpful to consider why these entities appear in such forms. Their primary basic state is in what may be termed a 'light body.' Not easy to describe in words, it is nebulous like a fine mist, being a whirl or vortex of energy in constant motion. It glows with colored light, sometimes one single color, sometimes two or more, which do not mix but remain separate like the colors in a rainbow. It frequently changes color and is often covered with a multitude of fine curved lines. These are usually golden but can be of other colors. They appear to flow like liquid in a pipe, forming continually changing patterns of incredible beauty. These light bodies differ from each other in size and brilliance, varying from pale pastel shades to strong bright colors. All are beautiful, pure, and luminous, glowing with inward radiance. They may be regarded as whirls of energy, but energy with intelligence. It is possible to see and to communicate with these light bodies.

"However, in these bodies the elementals are unable to work with the denser forces and counterparts of the plants. They must take on an etheric body, possibly built of the material from the etheric shell of the Earth. In his myths, legends, and fairy tales, man has depicted a vast gallery of what he has referred to as 'supernatural' beings. To what extent these beings were the product of man's own creative imagination or the result of inspiration from an outside source is difficult to determine. Suffice to say that there exists a vast reservoir of 'thought forms' produced by the existence and persistence of these tales. Often thought and talked about, these forms have been preserved both orally, as in the older days, and in print. Thus, an elemental entity wishing to assume a body can 'put on' any of these thought forms and then appear personified as that particular being —Greek or Norse god, elf, gnome, faun, fairy, and so on.

"Many of these beings think that by taking on such forms known to man they will be recognized for what they are and are disappointed because this does not happen; but instead they are not seen and are subsequently disbelieved. They have become used to this but still have hope. Man is much less sensitive now than he once was when such contact was possible and even easy. No doubt, man had to lose his sensitivity and awareness in order to develop his intellect. The time has now come when the sensitivity is gradually being renewed, a time in which man will retain his intellect while heightening his awareness.

"In myths and legends these beings are frequently shown as behaving in a very human manner and expressing human emotion, which the real entities would not display. The tellers or writers of the tales have 'personalized' the being, and the entity using the form can take on humanlike behavior as well as the form. This is illustrated by an amusing experience I had in the Botanic Gardens. I was sitting on a seat under some trees watching with delight a group of gnomes gamboling about round a tree, obviously enjoying themselves, chasing each other and rolling over in the grass with shouts of laughter. I thought how like fat children they were. Immediately one of them turned around and glared at me. He came quickly over to where I was sitting, put his hands on his hips, and looking very cross, said, 'I'm not fat.' Turning, he walked back to the others with dignity. Humanlike behavior? Of course he was right. According to his own kind he was not fat—but gnomes do tend to be tubby.

"It is important to realize that though Pan can appear in such form, he is not a being restricted to one place. The word 'pan' means 'all' and 'everywhere.' Pan is a universal energy, a cosmic energy, which is constantly found throughout the whole of nature. He could appear personified in many different places at the same time and should never be thought of as restricted to a corner of the garden, lurking behind a tree in the wood, or sitting on a hilltop behind a gorse bush. The description of my meeting with Pan might give this impression, but care should be taken not to fall into this limiting trap. Think of Pan as everywhere all the time.

"It is important for the future of mankind that belief in the Nature Spirits and their god Pan is reestablished and that they are seen in their true light and not misunderstood.

These beings, in spite of the innumerable outrages man has committed against nature, are only too pleased to help him if he will seek and ask for their cooperation. They must be believed in with complete sincerity and faith. They must never be taken for granted and should be given love and thanks for the work they do. With such cooperation, what could be achieved would seem miraculous to many. It has been sought and asked for at Findhorn, and the results have been given."

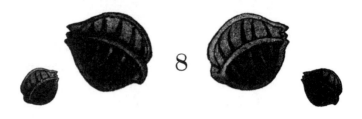

8

The Wizard Meets the Elf King

0

But perhaps the most mysterious thing he ever said about it was this. I was questioning him on the subject . . . and had incautiously said, "Of course, I realize it's all rather too vague for you to put into words," when he took me up rather sharply by saying, "On the contrary, it is words that are vague. The reason why the thing can't be expressed is that it's too definite for language."

—C. S. Lewis, *Voyage to Venus*

Crombie and Peter approached a thickly wooded glen looking for a path through the undergrowth. The surface was overgrown—trees were intertwined and gnarled; ivy was locked and wrapped around the trunks. The leaves glistened. The dampness came up through their shoes. Each twig and leaf quivered as if the two human beings walking in their midst had created a stifled tension. Everything seemed to be waiting, distinctly aware of their presence.

The ground was wet and slippery, and they were moving very slowly. Crombie had gone ahead, for he felt he had found the trail and was now following it. He had to step over fallen trees and around bushes that tugged at his coat and pulled at his pants. There was no easy way up the path.

Crombie had visited Rosemarkie as a child of four. During the Easter holidays in 1903, Roc's mother and father came to the Black Isle and took him to see the Faerie Glen, a place of great natural beauty which was being carefully maintained as a part of a large estate. He couldn't believe what he saw now: sixty years of abuse and abandonment. It looked as though the trees had made a pact with the undergrowth to exclude human beings. The thickets were practically impenetrable, and behind them were fences of fallen trees. A gray mist clogged the air.

Moss mounds and lichen groves dotted the forest floor, suspending round droplets of water in their crevices—a bejeweled archipelago in an undulant sea of mist that swirled and eddied about his feet. Crombie was concerned, looking around as if there were something that he couldn't quite catch, something appearing in the corner of the eye that vanished when he turned to discover what it was. He walked behind a clump of rhododendrons and reappeared on the other side, looking worried. Peter knew then that something was wrong, so he quickly moved forward toward Roc.

Crombie turned back to Peter and held up his hand to halt his progress. He then stepped behind a tree and could no longer be seen. Peter found a stump, brushed the surface clean, and sat down to wait. It was damp, but they had been walking all day and he was anxious to sit down.

Crombie moved forward slowly, stopping every few feet. He was entering a very uncomfortable atmosphere. Each succeeding step brought him deeper into a darkness and negativity. It was a black mist that swirled about the gleaming leaves. His energy was draining, and all seventy years weighed upon him in full. The feeling became almost unbearable, but Roc's determination to continue remained resolute. He thought he heard a sound or rustling, but when he stopped to listen, all was silent.

Again he saw something moving up ahead and stopped and waited. Whatever it was, it had stopped. As he stepped around a large beech tree he saw it again darting to the right. He wheeled around, but there was nothing.

Dew-encrusted strands hung upon a motionless wall of

green. A drop of water fell, a leaf jiggled. It stopped and blended back into the spatial silence. Roc moved no farther. Something was there. He would wait. There was no sound at all. A strong and powerful odor of earth and old pine needles rose from the forest floor, an acid smell of ten billion soil creatures expiring into the late afternoon air. Roc was sucking it in and began feeling oddly alive and aware. His body became rooted and still, a thick fibrous cellulose stalk shooting forth from a black earthen belly. He could feel thick colloidal milk rising, twisting, nodule-born jelly sugars oozing up. The protoplasmic cellsap born in the womb below was swelling in the emergent leaves of his hands. He was the stem enclasped and sheathed in thin diaphanous coils, sinuate and virgin pale, unfolding in the soft light.

The green mosaic became fused with his vision, and from the dense emerald world he began to see an image before him. Separating from the buds, stems, and leaves, two figures were standing before him. Green cloaks and hoods, green skin, green hands, green eyes shining, two bows notched with arrows, green arrows pointed right at him. They were three feet tall, and there was a grim beauty about them. Their faces were expressionless, but from one came a voice that pierced the air: "Mortal man, do not dare to come any farther. This is now our territory."

Roc was startled by the hostility and fierceness of his voice. "I'm a friend of Pan's . . . and I'm a friend of all Nature Beings. I come to you with love in my heart."

"We have no love for you, man," said the second elf. "Go back to where you came from and leave us in peace."

They stood still and tense, their arrows pointed at Roc. In his life he had heard enough tales about those who run afoul of the "Little People" to know this was a serious matter.

"I believe in you and want your friendship and help."

"That may be so, but this is our stronghold. We want no mortals here."

Roc wondered how to reply. He could now feel the presence of Pan behind him but knew Pan was not going to intervene.

The elves looked steadily at Roc, then lowered their bows and turned away to confer. Presently they turned back to Roc and indicated that he could proceed, but *that* man over there on the stump was to remain seated where he was.

They stepped aside and let Roc pass. He went on for about a dozen yards to where the gently rising path reached a level point. Roc decided it was better to turn back.

Before leaving, he looked at the elves again. The hostility written in their faces was new to him. Something terrible must have happened here. As he looked around and saw the damage to the glen, the fallen trees and the cut-off stumps, it became obvious that man was that terrible thing. The hostility was not vicious; it was more of protective grief. This was a refuge, their place of isolation and retreat. It was all they had left, and soon it would perish as well.

Roc returned to where Peter was sitting and motioned him on without saying anything. They walked back to the car in silence and then drove to their hotel. Roc was still puzzled. It was the first time he had encountered hostility from the Nature Spirits, and he began to question some of his earlier assumptions about them. Suddenly it was more complex. Their expression wasn't sinister, but it was very queer, and there was a quality of desperation in their faces and voice—defiant desperation. He had to go back.

After dinner that night, Roc excused himself and went to the Faerie Glen alone. Through the thick brush, he retraced his steps. A nearly full moon painted silver wisps on the mists. Branches were starkly outlined against the luminous sky, and again there was an absolute stillness; not a sound broke the spell. The going was even more difficult at night, but he found the path again and picked his way up and over the obstacles. The silence around him was filled with living presences which were watching. He stopped where he had encountered the two before and waited. They weren't there. But he was sure he was to wait.

Roc's white crown of hair shone like snow against the moon shadows. The forest seemed to move forward to enclose and trap him within. Once again he could feel his perceptions changing. His body became rooted and one with the earth, his hands tingled, his arms felt like enormous branches hanging down from a trunk. He was naked, and the woolen pullover and breeches felt more like moss or fur. Every tree appeared humanly alive, and what had been motionless now seemed to move slowly, almost imperceptibly. With the same rhythmic motion, he turned his head, looking at every moving tree around him silhouetted against the sky. He acknowledged each with a slight nod. When he stopped turning, he saw to his left a huge massive tree that was moving more than imperceptibly. What had appeared to be a trunk was a towering figure. What had looked like silvery reflections were gleaming eyes set into blackness. Behind it, the white moon froze in the sky. Neither said anything.

When Roc turned back again, there was before him the green luminescence of the two elves. There were no arrows, and they greeted him. Roc was led up a path which was now free and clear. They came to the top of the hill where the path widened out. Ahead of him, down in a glade, there was a glow and emanation of light which grew brighter as he approached. A stream lay beyond the fringe of trees, and the distant sound of a waterfall could be heard.

When he reached the end of the path, he beheld a great assembly of Nature Spirits, moving, flying, and shimmering. In the center of the glade on a small hillock sat a creature four feet tall. The figure motioned to Roc and indicated that he was to come to the center. He descended into a sea of glowing and flickering phosphorus. Spirits were brilliantly alight in the air like stars, bluish green opalescence, darting about and hovering, gently descending to the ground before shooting up into the air again. All were agitated and excited as Roc walked toward the center, their attention fixed on this one old white-haired man who dared to enter.

The figure in the middle was an elfin creature. All the beings around him closed in, moving as if they were one organism. There was a sound like the strains of music, a muted tuning of strings and flutes rising and falling in drones like a wind in the reeds. The figure appeared enormously powerful. The elf rose to greet Roc and, pointing to a hump in the ground, invited him to sit before him. The elves and Nature Spirits watched with interest and curiosity as he seated himself. Roc was aware of waves of hostility. He felt vulnerable, a stranger in another world, a prisoner in the hands of the little people.

The elf king stared at Roc with cold piercing eyes. The hostility was increasing. The murmurs sank into a heavy silence. The elf king's voice was hard: "Man, we have no understanding of you. You upset the balance of nature, destroy the animals, turn land to desert, cut and burn the large trees, maim the landscape, blasting great wounds in the hills and mountains, slashing the living earth so that it will not heal.

"You pollute everything beneath you and everything above you. Everywhere you go is fouled and destroyed. Are you so stupid that you cannot realize you are destroying yourself?

"You cannot destroy us, for we are immortal and indestructible. But we care about this planet, we love it, it is our home and abode. It was once beautiful. Can you blame us if we consider you a parasite on the face of the Earth?

"You! You have the effrontery to ask for our cooperation! Cooperation in what? In the devastation of our strongholds? Our sacred places? Our dwellings? Justify your request! Explain yourself! What is the meaning of your life, Man?"

There was tremendous excitement among the crowd of

elves, and a murmuring broke out like the sound of the wind in the trees rising in volume before an approaching storm. The hostility rose and beat down like a physical force.

Roc felt a thousand eyes upon him, eyes of beings he had never before seen, beings he might never again see, a vast multitude for which he had no words. Until a year ago, he had never dreamed of a Nature Spirit. Now, everywhere he went, Nature Spirits appeared. First in Edinburgh Gardens, then at Attingham and Iona, and now hardly a week passed when he was not aware of their presence or held converse with them. He began to identify with them more than Man. Was it madness after all? And here he was asked to explain Man, his actions, his ruthless destruction of his surroundings, and he felt as distant and remote from Man as they did. Yes, who was this Man, this creature that swarmed over the Earth? What was he doing to himself? What possible meaning could there be to the entropic decay of life and consciousness? He himself was neither Man nor Nature Spirit. His contacts with that realm had left him in a place of nonattachment; yet he was totally dedicated to life.

Roc stood and faced the elves. He began by admitting that the accusations were true, but were only part of the picture—the dark part. He did not attempt to justify or excuse these outrages, the only excuses being ignorance, stupidity, and lack of love and care.

"Mankind is not evil. The majority of the inhabitants of this Earth are peace-loving and kind and want to live in friendship with all. This is the truth. It is easy to see bad deeds. It is less easy to see good ones. But to be fair, you must try to do so. There are many people every bit as distressed as I am at the outrages committed against nature, at the cruelty and destruction inflicted on the animal kingdom, at the exploitation of the plant kingdom and the raping of the mineral kingdom. On behalf of those who are wantonly destroying the earth, I can say nothing. But there are people now who want to bring peace to Earth and to the Nature Kingdom."

The figures had listened intently, and now in the starlit hush he could feel the tension lessen.

"We have heard of one called Jesus who wanted to bring peace. What did mankind do to him? You destroy those who would change your accustomed way of life."

Roc paused for a moment and thought about what the elf had said.

"He is destroyed only in one form. He is reborn and lives in another, a level in which we all live. Jesus was a teacher, a divine being, and there have been others as well. No parasite could bring forth such teachers and teachings.

"Man is seeking fundamental truths, and in his search he has temporarily forgotten God. Continue to be patient and tolerant with man. You are disbelieved now, but more and more are beginning to accept your existence. Only deeds satisfy. It is up to mankind to convince you that we care, we respect and honor nature and its kingdoms. I ask that you be fair to us. Help us." Roc stopped and waited for a reply.

"We have listened and accept what you have said."

Roc paused and thought about the next question, wondering whether to ask it or not. "May I ask a question?" he finally ventured.

"I will answer if it is allowable," replied the elf king.

"Could you destroy mankind if you wanted to?"

The elf king sat motionless and looked quietly into Roc's eyes. "Easily," he said.

"How?"

"The vital force in all that grows would cease."

"That would mean the end!" was Roc's half question, half statement. "Is that in accordance with God's will?"

"If Man goes too far he will destroy himself—he doesn't need us. He has the means of doing so, and he has free will.

We do what we must, but we cannot break cosmic laws which are God's laws."

Roc looked at the elf king. "I do not believe that will ever happen. Man is turning within. More and more people seek to understand. It will take time, but know that everything is now changing."

A smile crept across the elfin face. Roc realized it had taken an enormous strain for this being to remain serious all this time. Elves had always appeared dignified to Roc, but never had he seen them without mirth and humor. The elfin figure was like a child who had been pouting but now began to laugh despite himself.

"Well, we will do nothing to hurt you. But if Man enters where he is not wanted, or acts to destroy, then do not blame us if we play tricks. . . ." And the last word had not left his lips before he started fading into the hillock and the lights dimmed, the beings disappeared, and Roc could see the two elves who had brought him there dancing right over the crest into the dark forest, and he was alone . . . in the moonlight.

Peter met Crombie in 1965, and during the following year they traveled through England, Scotland, and Wales. Peter and Roc became a two-man delegation to the world of Nature Spirits: Peter the chauffeur and navigator, Roc the diplomatic representative of man.

At that time, Peter was just making himself known to the clubby and convoluted world of British spiritual groups. Into this tight-knit and predominantly upper-middle-class coterie, Peter came blundering during a "New Age" conference at Attingham Park. It was a conference called to gather all the New Age groups under one roof for the "first time," to charter a course on the rough seas of advanced social disease. It was the *crème de la crème*, just the thirty very "in" souls gathered to the fold by Sir George Trevelyan, and Peter was not invited. The tweeds and chiffon watched as this brash and tanned gardener from the North gate-crashed their well-arranged conference, talking about Findhorn and God's guidance. They could almost smell the pigmuck in the cracks of his shoes. Peter was glorying in this thick and heady air of the New Age.

Suggestions were taken by the chairman for drawing up a charter for the New Age. Peter was incredulous, stunned, quivering with indignation. He shot up from his chair and spoke to stony-faced silence: "We are practicing what is being talked about. We are building a new age community at Findhorn right now. We are not talking about it. You can't make a charter for the New Age. There are no blueprints. We have been told by God through Eileen that we are to live in the moment, guided by God. It is His plan, not ours. Let it be revealed through Him. Patterns are revealed when looking back, not when looking ahead." And he sat down. Silent shock.

Thunderation. Who let this outspoken upstart with that Brobdingnagian voice into the conference? Air Marshal Sir Victor Goddard, the second-highest ranking officer in the Royal Air Force, slowly rose. He stared at Peter and then addressed him: "Would you like to say a few words and illuminate us all as to how you expect to finance your new age community?"

Peter faltered. He had come down to the conference on fourteen shillings and a prayer. He was flat broke. He had set off from Findhorn in an old car with half a tank of gas and a few sandwiches. He didn't even know how he was going to drive back to Findhorn. Finances? There were none. "It's quite simple, sir. One gives up everything for God. You put him first, in the faith and conviction that all one's needs will be perfectly met from His perfect and abundant supply." Peter sat down again to a prolonged hush. Ta ta and cheerio! Don't come to us when you're bankrupt and the taxman tows your caravan away. Some wrote Peter off as a proper fool.

But when Crombie met Peter, he couldn't write him off so easily. He saw Peter as naïve, yes, but it wasn't quite that simple. There was something positively sincere and endearing about this man; his faith in Eileen's guidance was childlike and inspiring. He was carrying out what he thought to be God's instructions to the letter, a spiritualized RAF man right down to his bunions.

And when Peter first met Crombie, he realized that he was meeting someone who commanded complete respect. Was it because no one knew anything about him? It wasn't just his age, the white hair, or the clear and authoritative voice, but there was a definitiveness that made people listen, and Peter listened too. Spiritual groups hounded Roc to join, but he never did. Crombie came to talks, lectures, meetings, but he only listened—he never joined.

When the two met, it was like a Jesuit meeting a knight errant. Roc was quiet, keen, and contemplative, hardly speaking or moving. Peter was charging about setting fires, knocking over windmills, and saying outrageous things to people who "knew better." Perhaps when they met, each saw in the other something he lacked. For Roc, it was youth, leadership, and energy; for Peter, it was the tempering of age and a deep incisive perception of the invisible world.

The friendship between Peter and Roc deepened. When Peter could get away from the garden, the two of them took trips around the British Isles visiting points of natural or historical interest. From the experience in Rosemarkie and many other similar experiences, Roc began to sense the vastness of what he called the Kingdom of the Nature Spirits, and with that realization came the awareness of how deep was the rift between man and them.

Peter saw nothing, but he had a knack for finding places where Roc could encounter concentrations of nature beings. The elementals varied from place to place, an infinite variety of beings whose color, form, and shape changed with the terrain and the seasons.

To this day Roc has no explanation of why he stumbled across this world, or why he was "chosen." But once contact had been established, his understanding and knowledge of this world grew in leaps and bounds. He would sit down in the woods by himself, or sometimes in Edinburgh Gardens, and talk for hours with these beings, asking questions of them. Far from being wary, they were delighted that someone showed interest in them. They would crowd around Roc, as much a novelty to them as they were to him. Oh, they had seen plenty of human beings, but they had assumed that communication and understanding between the two kingdoms had been cut off long ago, and so they had given up trying—just as we don't try to look for them.

In a sense, our "reality" as living human beings is now a fairy tale for them, or a "human tale," actually. They look back with fondness on the stories of an olden race of men living on the earth who could enter their realm with ease and grace, men and women who lived with them, talked with them, and worked with them. If we think they are a myth or legend, so be it, but according to them, real human beings are also a myth and legend. They are not sure now what it is that walks the earth. People they are, but people who seem to have gone amuck. Civilization through their eyes is one endless disaster. They tell stories and ask questions which suggest that their horror is mixed with a great deal of humor. Kurmos was astonished to watch metal boxes with people in them almost run down other people. They are mystified that we think knowledge comes from books and artifacts. Roc in fact could not even explain to them what it was that men "got" from books. Wars completely baffle them.

They have explained to Roc that their work is solely with the plant and mineral kingdom. It is a formative role, taking the energy the Devas channel to plants and molding and fusing this energy with the growth of the plant. It is an energy we might call "life force."

Roc is often asked what is the use of Nature Spirits. They may exist, but do we really need them? Won't plants grow anyway? From what Roc has learned, the answer to that question may be a qualitative one. Plants may grow, but they won't grow well. Wherever he goes, he feels that the Nature Spirits are withdrawing from plants, farms, and gardens. The effect of their withdrawal is already being felt.

Crombie gives the analogy of children and parents. Nature Spirits are not the parents of plants, but their role is similar. The plants draw nourishment from the soil, air, and water, interacting within a complex relationship of bacteria, microorganisms, and animals. A child is nourished by foods which are usually given to him by his mother. But it has been observed that if you take children from their parents and put them in an institution with many other children where they receive nothing but their "needs," namely food, clothing, and shelter, those children suffer emotional and spiritual deprivation. They are not happy and often become extremely aggressive or introverted. Their behavior is antisocial, and in spite of eating proper food, they can become physically weak and suffer ill health as if their will to live was very slight indeed. They die more easily; their contribution to the greater fabric of society is minimized, and often it is a destructive contribution. A child suffers similarly even within the context of a home where the mother and father do not give him love.

In this analogy, orphanages are the factory farms of agribusiness, mechanical and chemicalized forestry, or any situation where plants are manipulated, forced, and exploited for our ends. In these situations the Nature Spirits have withdrawn. And so we are witnessing a weakening of the plant life, an erosion of its "will" to live. Such plants are becoming sterile, can grow only under ideal conditions, and are subject to large-scale infestation by insects.

The point that the Nature Spirits insist upon to Roc is a rather extraordinary one. The energy which they channel into the plants is a "vital" energy. In other words, it is an energy which is necessary for life, and as it is slowly withdrawn, it is withdrawn from man as well. Of course, they do not express it this way. Theirs is a much simpler statement: Unless there is cooperation between men and plants, man destroys himself. That is why they are so shocked at man's behavior. Why is man destroying himself? To them it looks as deliberate and planned as anything ever has been. The organization, skill, and energy which man is devoting to this very complex act of self-destruction is completely flabbergasting to them. Doesn't man know? How could he not? He is working so hard at it! He is devoting every ounce of his strength to it! Surely he is doing it on purpose! But Roc keeps saying no. Really, they don't know, they do not really mean to do what they are doing. These statements are greeted with the same incredulity and astonishment from the Nature Spirits that we accord to Roc's statement of their very existence.

Roc lives in a nature that is more "alive" than others would probably concede. It is a nature that can respond with a will, not just an automatic predetermined response. The collective conscious of Nature as expressed through the aspect of Nature Spirits is not as attached to Earth as are plants, animals, and rocks. It can freely leave it and may do just that.

Roc sees mankind enacting the biblical edict to exercise dominion over everything without understanding the spirit of the word. Dominion does not mean to dominate by force, to make things do what you think they *ought* to do. Neither does it mean to force or exploit something, or to distort its impulses for self-gain through manipulation. To have dominion means to understand completely, to have sympathy, to love, to enter into a state of wholeness and perfect harmony with all of creation. The Nature Spirits are tolerant to a degree, to a very great degree. They will accept the most appalling outrages, because they are closer to that infinite wisdom and understanding than we are at present.

But instead of revolting against the excesses of mankind, they are rather inclined to slip away, much as the consciousness of the child abandoned in an orphanage slips into other worlds. The Nature Spirits are simply disappearing. From the experience at Rosemarkie and many others, Roc has become acutely aware of the deep rift between man and these Spirits. Having already withdrawn from farms and most gardens, the only place they can now be found is in the hidden and deep recesses of the forest, or in wild moors. And what concerns Roc is that they may already be irretrievably lost to us, their forces withdrawn.

Roc was introduced to the Findhorn Garden and brought with him this intimate contact with the Nature Kingdom and Pan. He sought their help and cooperation in making the gardens an example of what could be accomplished among Man, the Devas, and the Nature Spirits. He was told by Pan that a "wild area" should be established in the garden to serve as a sanctuary for the Nature Spirits, an area that was allowed to grow naturally without any tending. To this day, the wild area behind the original caravan is covered by gorse, broom, and scrub pine.

The garden had been used mainly for growing food, but after Roc arrived, Eileen received guidance that it was to be a place of great beauty, that they were to plant trees, shrubs, and flowers. They acquired two more acres of land and two bungalows and began this new phase of the garden. Although the barren soil was considered to be quite inadequate for growing deciduous trees, Roc sought aid from Pan, who promised that all trees and shrubs would do well in this soil.

At the end of April, very late in the season for planting, Peter went to a nursery to buy some trees. "Looking around the nursery, I was inspired to get a large chestnut tree, together with an assortment of other trees and shrubs. These were duly planted in the sandy soil, and a dry summer followed. Pan, however, kept his promise. The growth of the chestnut tree averaged fourteen inches, an astonishing amount in view of the adverse conditions under which it was growing. The growth and color of the flowers in the new herbaceous borders, planted in pure sand and nothing else, since all the compost had been used up, was truly remarkable. One delphinium grew to a height of eight feet and had enormous blossoms. The colors of all the flowers shone with a scintillating quality. In fact many of our visitors told us that they had never seen such a uniformly high standard in all sections in any garden before, and they were at a loss to understand it in view of the poor quality of the soil and the northern climate. It certainly wasn't due to my experience as a gardener!"

Findhorn was an experiment in the cooperation among three kingdoms: Man, as embodied by Peter; the Devas, as communicated through Dorothy; and the Nature Spirits, as understood through Roc. And as an experiment it was not long before the first disaster struck.

Near the "wild place" that had been established for the Nature Spirits, Peter planted a small orchard of apple and pear trees. Within a year, the gorse bushes had overgrown their original area and were starting to crowd out the fruit trees. Peter meant to cut them back in the winter, but had forgotten. In the spring, he asked a young man who was helping him if he would cut back the gorse, which was then in full flower with bright yellow masses of blossoms. The young man, who had learned much about Devas and Nature Spirits, demurred, but Peter insisted. Peter told him that as long as he explained to the Nature Spirits that the gorse was preventing the growth of food, it would be all right. The gorse was cut. Dorothy almost left the community. It was butchery to cut them in flower, she said. Peter didn't understand. People cut lawns—is that butchery? I am Man; I just can't sit back and let nature "take over." Roc was in Edinburgh at the time, but knew immediately that something had gone wrong at Findhorn.

He came up that weekend and asked Peter what had gone wrong, what had he done? Peter said he hadn't done anything and didn't even connect Roc's visit with the gorse bushes.

Roc began to walk around to see if he could discover what this "feeling" was that he was picking up. He left the garden to go to the beach. The path from Findhorn winds through a profusion of gorse bushes, and as he looked behind him, he could see a lot of little elves following him. They were clamoring about and seemed to be in an absolute frenzied state. What was the man doing? they wanted to know. Why has he cut off our homes? We told you it wouldn't work; we can't work with Man when he does stupid things like that. Those blossoms are our homes. They were leaving the garden to man, he could do what he wanted, they would go back to the wild places.

Roc knew what had happened. The gorse had been cut in blossom. Since Peter hadn't told him, he had to learn it from the elves. He sat down and softly began to explain to them about Man. Yes, wasn't he ignorant? So ignorant, but Man can learn, too. Roc apologized for the incident, explaining over and over that here Man was learning to cooperate with them, and that there were bound to be some mistakes. Could they understand that?

They could understand, and they returned to the garden.

The following year brought the most serious test of the strength of the forces which operated in the garden. The previous winter three more bungalows were constructed directly in the face of the north wind, surrounded by sand and gravel. Peter saw an advertisement in the Sunday paper from a nursery in the south of England. They were offering a dozen varieties of deciduous trees at an unusually low price. It was a gamble, but Peter went ahead and ordered six hundred, including some beech trees which were to be planted in the form of a hedge enclosing the whole of the garden. The order was dispatched, and on May 16, after nine days en route, the trees arrived, dried out and shriveled. The change in climate from the warmth of the south to the cold of the north had left them in shock. Into the pure sand they were planted, during a bitingly cold gale from the northeast. Dorothy and Roc were both asked to seek help and cooperation, for without it surely all the trees would die. Dorothy received from the Landscape Angel that they were *including all these new trees and shrubs in a solid downpour of radiation, a wall of it, for they must indeed be stabilized and kept immersed in the life's elements. . . .*

Roc could see this wall of energy being used by the Nature Spirits, especially around the roots. Roc communicated with them all, thanking them for their effort in this cause. Slowly, the trees came to life. New leaves emerged to replace the dead brown ones, and they began to stand erect. Not one of them died. Peter had asked some amateur and professional gardeners what the chances were of success with these trees. All agreed that the chances were virtually nil, yet the experiment was working. A great feeling of exaltation and joy grew among everyone in the garden. They knew now that they could demonstrate that in cooperation and harmony with these Kingdoms, miracles could be accomplished.

The Landscape Angel expressed the spirit of the new garden: *There is a world to be redeemed, and all forces are needed for that purpose. Unity and cooperation are the keynotes. We are with you as you are aligned to God, and the forces we deal with are absolutely essential to your life. Your bodies could not exist without the work we do. Man can no longer rape his worlds . . . or the whole cannot continue. Life is a whole. Harmony has been ordained throughout the Universe. Man will play his unique part, and thus the world may then continue . . . all of it. We are part of this great chain. You join us in your wider-ranging fields so that His will be done on Earth to create God's finest fruits.*

9

Lords and Ladies

Sir George Trevelyan, son of the aristocratic cabinet minister Sir Charles Trevelyan, and nephew of the historian G. M. Trevelyan, was raised in the highly stimulating environment of a British upper-class household which was the model of "culture," where afternoon tea in the library was followed by poetry. Emerging from his family home in Northumbria a scholar and devoted educator, he taught at Gordonstoun, counting among his students Prince Philip, and later pioneered adult education in England.

Sir George remembered the brash and youthful Peter Caddy who spoke at his conference in Attingham and decided to find out for himself if this man spoke the truth. During his tour of Findhorn, he was bowled over by the growth he saw in the garden. He knew Peter was no gardener, and he saw what the soil was like, but he tasted the abundant vegetables and saw the vibrancy of the flowers, and yet here it was only early spring! Realizing that something was going on and determined to get to the bottom of it, he fired questions at Peter about the garden.

Peter had until this time said nothing to anyone about Devas or Nature Spirits. He felt comfortable working with these forces, but he did not know how others would feel. When questioned, he ascribed the phenomenality of the garden to compost and organic methods. Sir George wouldn't buy it. He demanded an explanation, and Peter finally capitulated, telling the inquisitive visitor the real story behind the garden. Sir George, as an avid student of Rudolf Steiner, fully understood. Steiner had founded his Bio-Dynamic methods of agriculture on his investigations of "etheric" formative forces, and the demonstration here in northern Scotland was not a repetition of theory, but a conscious application of the knowledge of these forces.

After his visit, Sir George wrote the following memo:

This memorandum is the presentation of a phenomenon that calls for investigation. At Easter in 1968, I stayed with Peter Caddy, who lives with a small group of friends on the Caravan Site at Findhorn Bay in Moray. Their caravans are surrounded by a lovely garden. There were daffodils and narcissi as beautiful and large as I have ever seen, growing in beds crowded with other flowers. I was fed on the best vegetables I have ever tasted. A young chestnut eight feet high stood as a central feature, bursting with astonishing power and vigour. Fruit trees of all sorts were in blossom. In short, it is one of the most vigorous and productive of small gardens I have ever seen, with a quality of taste and colour unsurpassed. Many species of broad leaved trees and shrubs are planted and thriving, yet the caravan site is on the landward slope of windswept sand dunes. The soil is simply sand and gravel on which grows spiky grass. Exactly opposite them is Culbin Sands where after fifty years' growth, conifers have rooted and held the dunes so that tough grass can now begin to root. Other folk on the caravan site, seeing the lovely burgeoning around their neighbor's caravans, put in cabbages and daffodils which came up as miserable specimens. Caddy claims to have grown a 42 lb. cabbage!

He brings in straw and farmyard manure and makes compost. Some beds are liberally mulched and composted, though some seem to thrive with only a modest amount mixed into the dusty sandy soil. When I was there he was in the process of planting young beeches to make a hedge. Beeches simply do not grow on soil like this, nor should any of the many other trees now thriving on the plot. Good basic organic husbandry is going on, but what at once struck me was that this is not an adequate explanation. Caddy began this garden in 1963, never having sown a seed in his life. The flower garden is less than a year old —the splendid show I saw is its first spring blooming.

I make no claim to be a gardener but I am a member of the Soil Association, interested in organic methods and have seen enough to know that compost and straw mulch alone mixed with poor and sandy soil is not enough to account for the garden. There must be, I thought, a Factor "X" to be taken into consideration. What is it?

I pressed Caddy for his explanation. Here we have to take the plunge and what follows will appeal to some and be unacceptable to others. Caddy's dedicated group are living a God-centered life. His wife, Eileen, makes a daily contact at the highest spiritual level which brings very direct advice and teaching. Another colleague, Dorothy, is a sensitive. When they were prompted to start gardening in this unpromising terrain they at once came up against difficulties through inexperience, but conceived a novel way of getting help and advice. They knew of the world of the Devas, who might be described as the architects of the plant world. So they decided to seek help and Dorothy quite simply, in meditation, asked the Pea Deva for advice.

Gardeners with green fingers are, of course, working unconsciously with the nature spirits through their sheer love of plants. What appears to be new at Findhorn is that here is a group of amateurs, starting gardening from scratch, using a direct mental contact with the Devic world and in fullest consciousness basing their work on this cooperation.

Another friend of Caddy's, closely in touch with the work there, is an older man whom they call Roc whose consciousness has opened to the elemental world. His ability to "talk" with these beings is therefore complementary to Dorothy's Deva contact and to Eileen's contact with the High Divine Source. This group together, with Caddy himself doing and directing the practical work, makes a balanced team to demonstrate this cooperation in action.

They are literally demonstrating that the desert can blossom as the rose. They also show the astonishing pace at which this can be brought about. If this can be done so quickly at Findhorn, it can be done in the Sahara. If enough men could really begin to use this cooperation consciously, food could be grown in quantity in the most infertile areas. There is virtually no limit if Factor "X" can be brought into play on top of our organic methods.

This phenomenon is so remarkable that it calls for open-minded and unprejudiced investigation. The challenge, I repeat, is that here something is happening which appears to be beyond normal methods of organic husbandry. It is not enough to write it off as the use of good compost. The quality of flowers and vegetables growing in the sand simply belies it and if anyone believes he can achieve these results by normal methods, let him try in the next sand dune.

The memo was sent to Lady Mary and Lady Eve Balfour of the Soil Association. The two sisters had cultivated a small landholding during World War I, a subsistence farm on which they cared for animals and grew garden vegetables. An odd thing for the favorite nieces of the former Prime Minister of England, but both had an unswerving bent for the land, particularly Lady Eve. They had volunteered for wartime service but were rejected. Knowing that food was important, they began searching for a bigger farm. Not only could they help the wartime effort by supplying food, but Lady Eve was anxious to try out the theories she had learned at University of Reading Agricultural School. The war ended before they found their land, but by then the urge to farm was too deeply embedded to be dislodged.

They had heard of a farm for sale near Ipswich called New Bells which sounded perfect for their needs. The owner was going to sell it in three days if they did not come immediately with an offer, so, because of a national railway strike, the Ladies Mary and Eve set out on a cart pulled by their pony Maisie, sleeping in stables along the way. They fell in love with New Bells and bought it straightaway and then almost lost it during the depression as they struggled with all their resources to keep it afloat. During this time Lady Eve first read books about organic farming and began experimenting with compost. In 1943, after ten years of research and practical experience, she wrote *The Living Soil,* which has since become a classic in its field. It is the result of years of comparative studies at New Bells and other farms of crops grown with artificial and natural fertilizers. The response to the book was so great that she formed the British Soil Association, using New Bells, later renamed Haughley, as its research center. The Soil Association and Lady Eve have become synonymous with organic horticulture, and her experience there has made her one of the leading authorities in the world.

It was Lady Mary, however, who first came to Findhorn:

My brief visit was in September 1968. The weather throughout was mild, grey and at times wet. Yet in retrospect I see that garden in brilliant sunshine without a cloud in the sky. This can only have been due to the extraordinary brilliance of the flowers in bloom. And they all seemed to be in bloom! The flower beds were a compact mass of colour and form in great variety. The effect was riotous, but weedless; free but harmonious. I stooped to handle and examine the soil, a thickish layer of half-ripe compost lay mulching the rather grimy, too fine sand below. To my eye and touch it was indeed pure sand of the most unpromising quality.

Feeling not a little awestruck, I turned from bed to bed, noting how cunningly these were placed around the human habitations (the caravans). These were scattered as though haphazard, breaking up the whole into a variety of attractive vistas as well as providing shady corners and some shelter from the sea gales.

At this point the Custodian joined me and we went to the kitchen garden. The soft fruit had been wonderful judging by the size and vigour of the plants; raspberries, blackberries, loganberries, grown as a windbreak on one side of the vegetable plot. On the further side, a cordon of fruit trees broke up the wind—many of them were loaded with fruit.

Even the most chemically-minded growers will admit that some folks have "green fingers"—folk that can break the rules and still make plants flourish. Why? How? Wouldn't we like to know! Could that be just what the gardeners at Findhorn are beginning to learn?

Break the rules? What rules? Peter was blessedly ignorant of the rules. He didn't know what could not be done. He was willing to try anything. The garden was rapidly growing into a botanical garden in many respects, for there was a multitude of plants, and the growth each year had been so rapid that five years seemed precious little time to explain it all.

Peter was not only ignorant of rules; he was somewhat ignorant of what was happening. He immersed himself so completely in his work that the phenomenal aspects of the garden didn't really strike him. Since he didn't know what the limits to growth were, nothing seemed to surprise him. Plants did not appear oversized, since he had nothing to compare them to. He did manage a visit to nearby Cawdor Castle and saw a vegetable garden that had been maintained for almost four hundred years, but it was a poor specimen of gardening with its artificial fertilizers sprinkled white on the surface and did not even compare with Findhorn. Neighbors did express astonishment at the garden, but Peter had no firm reality check.

After Lady Mary's visit, the word spread quickly among members of the Soil Association. "See Findhorn!" And it was the experts that finally helped Peter realize that the garden was truly special.

During the following winter, a Scotsman came to visit the garden. Old, but spry and quick on his feet, he had a shock of silver hair tucked under a tam-o'-shanter, a crooked walking stick, and a kilt. Professor R. Lindsay Robb, consultant to the Soil Association, had spent most of his eighty-odd years researching and studying soils all over the world. He had assumed agricultural posts with government and academic institutions in England, New Zealand, South Africa, Australia, Madagascar, and Libya, and his last post was as chief of the United Nations Food and Agricultural Organization in Costa Rica.

It was not the ideal time of the year to visit. There were practically no flowers, the vegetable garden was dormant, the trees were without leaves. Professor Robb told Peter that the soil, or sand actually, couldn't be worse because it contained almost no organic matter, a dustlike material that retained little moisture. But he wrote: "The vigor, health and bloom of the plants in this garden at midwinter on land which is almost barren powdery sand cannot be explained by the moderate dressings of compost, nor indeed by the application of any known cultural methods of organic husbandry. There are other factors. They are vital ones."

Lindsay Robb returned to the Soil Association and told the founder-secretary, Donald Wilson, the "King of Compost," that he must go to Findhorn. Donald Wilson hooked up his caravan and did precisely that. When he got there, he not only had a look at the garden but ended up building a ten-ton compost heap. After his visit, he wrote to Peter: "I had fondly imagined a quiet holiday in the sand dunes beside the sea, with occasional visits to the Findhorn Gardens. We hadn't a clue what we were in for. If we contributed in any way, it was nothing to what Findhorn contributed to us. I never wrote a letter, read a book, put a toe in the sea, or had any quiet holiday. I am still riotously happy and I cannot thank you enough."

The Magic. No matter how straight, noble, or scientific the visitor, Findhorn had a way of making lifetime friends. Agnostics came away accepting the power of Eileen's guidance. Horticultural experts came away baffled at the garden. Donald Wilson came for a seaside holiday and left ten days later having built huge compost heaps, working every step of the way with community members a third of his age.

As word spread, the stories of Findhorn began to put some people off. There was scoffing, negative rumors, and outright disbelief. Donald Wilson felt obliged to answer the remarks of one "well-known" personage who had never visited Findhorn when he saw a letter stating her frank incredulity:

At Findhorn a group of very fine people, after long training and much tribulation, have completely given up their own wills and property to obey the will of God utterly and instantly. I would dearly like to find the way to do the same, but am still groping. I have sought the truth and the way in many places but I have never before been sure that I have found it. Of course I may be wrong. The only way of "knowing" is the response inside oneself. "By their fruits shall ye know them." The fruits are those I have been looking for. Their relation to the soil is the right one, which twenty-five years in the Soil Association has taught me to know. Their relation to other people and their insistence on Love and Light and Life are the right ones . . . I think the chances of being wrong are small. I am sure others will find other right ways. For me it is this one. They proclaim that there is an inflow of energy on an increasing scale coming into the world, and that many people all over the world who are conscious of it are preparing for it and working for it. I know that many queer sects have said similar things many times in the past and may be saying so now. I find nothing queer, nothing exclusive at Findhorn. I do wish you could spend a week here and see for yourself, which would be so much better than anything I could write.

Other people devised ways of "testing" Findhorn. Reluctant husbands brought to Findhorn by their enthusiastic wives would stand with pursed lips, refusing to look at the gardens, prodded along by their garrulous mates who would extol the virtues of love and elves. One day when Peter saw a woman leading a Church of England minister through the flower beds, he came out to answer any questions. The minister turned to Peter and said he thought it was just a lot of nonsense—the whole garden was ridiculous. God didn't help gardeners in that way. As the man went on and on, it turned out he was one of the top experts on roses in England. Peter, knowing that everyone has a unique contribution to make to Findhorn, immediately asked the man to design a rose garden to go alongside the road. The man agreed and later sent Peter a plan which included the names of the exact varieties and where they were to be planted. Peter had to send south for them, and when winter arrived, they were duly planted. The following summer, the minister returned to find banks of roses leaning over the roadway and expressed his amazement: "I can't understand it! I really cheated when I did this design, for I included roses that I knew couldn't possibly grow in this climate and soil, and there they are, blooming as well as, if not better than, the rest of them."

Lady Eve Balfour finally came in 1970 to see for herself. Never will you meet a person who embodies the soil more than Lady Eve. Well into her seventies, she plows along with a will, dressed in deep browns and oranges, her ribboned beret rakishly tilted over one black-patched eye, the other roving around, taking in her environment. An astute judge of soils and compost, she may be the leading expert in her field, but in appearance she is right off the farm. While the name Lady Balfour may create an image of wealth, nobility, and social grace emanating from every cold-creamed pore, Lady Eve is closer to an incarnation of a work horse, her graying hair clipped neatly back like a mane. She is totally unattached to any dogma, a person who learns everything from nature, completely dedicated to the earth and the plants and creatures it nurtures, making friends wherever she goes and always working on the land.

"I agree completely with Lindsay Robb. I couldn't explain the garden there by compost. They weren't putting on poor compost, but the soil was very poor. Short on humus, it was the kind of soil that you normally need a tremendous amount of organic matter on, and they just did not have it. I have seen other gardens as good, on big estates going for hundreds of years attended by teams of gardeners, but never one better!

"And I have seen communities operating from the same overall theory of guidance, but the outstanding thing about Findhorn is the efficiency—you never saw wheels turn, yet it was all so beautifully done. The smooth way of running with a feeling of harmony made it frightfully convincing. That's what draws me back as well as the garden. Usually these groups are a muddle. Either they are efficient and lack the harmony or the other way around. I always feel so refreshed there, it recharges me. Findhorn is my place!"

The recognition of the garden by authorities, experts, and the miscellaneous elite came at a time when it was beginning to fade in dominance. Findhorn had always been based on guidance, God's word through Eileen. Despite Peter's authoritarian air, the power did not originate with him, but with the guidance. But people who visited the garden encountered Peter, not the guidance, and the increasing numbers of young freaks, hippies, and ex-druggies found him almost intolerable. Yet Findhorn became known as the "place to go," a spiritual center. The publication in 1968 of *God Spoke to Me* by Eileen sent out tendrils all over Britain and the world. The book's reputation spread by word of mouth, and orders for it steadily increased. With the orders came inquiries from people who wanted to come to stay, visit, or just to meet this woman. Others simply dropped in. They weren't coming to see the garden; many of them wouldn't know a buttercup from a daisy. They came to experience the tangible revelation that Eileen was receiving and that Peter was building into form. Peter's devotion to Eileen's inspiration kept him busy building a Sanctuary, more bungalows for guests and residents, a dining room and community center, a continuing stream of structures and buildings dedicated to the evolution of Findhorn as a center of "light," a center where souls could be transformed by the energies present in and around the community.

Those who come to Findhorn today are struck by the smiling faces, the inexhaustible reservoirs of joy, the giggles, the sensitivity, the sheer drop into giddiness and creative play that all are involved in, but in 1968 it was more like the requiem for the old rather than the heralding of the new. It was dead serious. Peter would stride around finding fault with everyone. There was nothing but endless work, from early in the morning until late at night. There was no music, no dancing, no "fun nights," and no picnics. This New Age was serious business: there was a job to be done. Young freaks escaping burnt-out lives in London were verbally thrashed by Peter for the slightest deviation from the rigid order and structure of the community. Few could see through the military stance to the soul beneath. They left, but more replaced them, and despite all odds, young people actually started to stay and integrate into the community.

Up until this influx of new blood, it was a spiritual cargo cult, waiting for something to happen. From the skies, through world events, or from within, they were waiting for that signal, that sign, the ineffable essence of a new "reality" that would tell them that the old was passing away and the New Age was beginning. Like many in the sixties, the "bomb" and nuclear holocaust was foremost on their minds. Would the button be pressed? Would the end be by fire and sickening diseases of radiation? Were they not to create a rural ark? An agricultural ark with food to live on and God to navigate by? Were not these the days spoken of by Matthew as the "birth pangs of a new age"? How could this be laughed about? Was there not work to do? Was not time short? Eileen's compassionate God of the dawn was balanced by Peter's Jehovah of the dusk. The world was falling apart, it was decaying, the end was near. What was needed was strong action, order, discipline, and positive thinking to bring the stalwart souls through the eye of the needle. Peter was the helmsman, the captain, the chief, the Moses of northern Scotland, and if people couldn't tolerate him, that was fine—they would be left behind.

But there was the Magic. In spite of all the outward and awkward forms of hierarchical consciousness, you could feel the Magic and Power in the air, from Peter and from Eileen. There was something frustratingly contradictory about the situation. Whoever wandered in was never turned away. All were welcome if there was room, but they had hardly woken up the following morning before they had to face the Chief. Some saw contrasted in Peter their own disordered and chaotic lives and left because they would not change. Others who gave up, gave in, and submitted to the thick overlay of authority on their lives were rewarded with glimpses into something else. Peter's rigid structure created a sense of freedom that few had known, a sense of total release, not to Peter and not even to Findhorn. The whole emphasis on God was so straight and to the point that some people walked right in and out the same day. It was like looking at a searchlight up close. Peter was not the light; he was the parabolic mirror shining it right into the pits of your eyeballs. If it didn't burn you, it felt good. Burning came from resistance. Findhorn's yoga was in intensive karma yoga, and though the garden received its fair share of the energy, it had started to take on an entirely new role.

In 1970 the first booklet describing the garden was published and included pieces by Peter, Roc, and Dorothy. Pan, Devas, and Nature Spirits were discussed, and out it went to the sizable mailing list that Findhorn had accumulated. The publication of the book, eight years after their arrival, signaled a new role for the garden. Up to that point, the garden had been the "demonstration" of what man could do when he cooperated with the nature forces including the Devas and Elementals. It was to demonstrate the practical and aesthetic advantages of harmony and communion with these higher forces. The publication was the first in hundreds of years to recognize them, to praise them, and to point the way to a new relationship between man and nature. But subtly and without anyone's precognition, the garden was doing more than that. Important lessons had been learned in the garden, lessons drilled into Peter's head for seven summers, and they slowly suffused the greater consciousness of the community.

The plant world at Findhorn had been examined repeatedly by experts. And one after another said simply that the quality of the soil could not produce such vigorous and vital growth. So what did? What really was this Factor "X"? If it wasn't the soil that was doing it, what was? Marcel Vogel, an IBM research scientist, in his visit to the community some years later, said: "This garden isn't growing from the soil, only in the soil. The plants are fed by the consciousness of the community, and if that consciousness should falter or waver, if there should enter into the community disharmony, chaos, or disorder, they would not simply stop growing or diminish in radiance—they would shrivel and die."

The Nature Spirits were not saying to Peter: Look, see what we can do. They were saying: Look what *you* can do. We've always been able to do this, but only when man became conscious and aware, giving us love and understanding, could we create in this way. In other words, it was thought projected from Peter and others to the plant world that was creating the garden. *The universe begins to look more like a great thought . . . we ought rather to hail [the mind] as the creator and generator of the realm of matter.* The power of that idea was right in front of every member wherever he looked. It was waving in the summer breezes and poking its nose up through the winter snows. Hi! I'm a plant, and thanks to you, I'm the way I am. And so, without lectures, seminars, or buzz groups, the realization seeped in and around the consciousness of every person at Findhorn. Thought is reality. If this is what it does to plants, great God, what effect does it have on man?

Within man is potentially a far greater sensitivity than within a plant. Thoughts are real, alive and powerful—precursors of form and reality. The miraculous ways that needs were met in the community was a constant reminder of this, and lest anyone forgot, Peter reminded them almost daily. Yet within that awareness of the power of thought and ideation came the understanding of the role of love. You didn't tell a plant what to do; you entered into a communion and oneness with that plant. In that state of awareness and attunement both man and plant were transformed. After eight years, the first part of the experiment was over. The garden had taught Peter and Eileen a thousand lessons never to be forgotten. The purpose of Findhorn was not to be a garden. The bomb scare passed, world tensions eased, survival as a motive dropped quietly away. The Ark was anchored, the voyage was over, the initial experimentation finished.

The flowers continued to grow, the trees to flourish, the vegetables to nourish, but from thence forward, Findhorn was not to be a garden of plants, it was to be a garden of people. The lessons of the plant world were to be brought into the world of souls, spirits, and beings. And when this became obvious to Peter and Eileen, the souls, spirits, and beings began to pour in from all over the world. If Peter thought his hands were full when dealing with rows of radishes and rutabagas, he soon learned that working eighteen hours a day with vegetables was a cakewalk compared to nurturing the souls of nearly two hundred people.

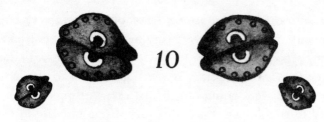

10

Lovers from Beyond
the Stars

"I gather," George continued, "that you have seen the reports I gave to the Island psychologist, so you know about the dreams."

"Yes: we know about them."

"I never believed that they were simply the imaginings of a child. They were so incredible that—I know this sounds ridiculous—they had to be based on some reality."

He looked anxiously at Rashaverak, not knowing whether to hope for confirmation or denial. The Overlord said nothing. . . .

"We were worried, but not really alarmed at first. Jeff seemed perfectly normal when he woke up and his dreams didn't appear to bother him. And then one night"—he hesitated and glanced defensively at the Overlord. "I've never believed in the supernatural: I'm no scientist, but I think there's a rational explanation for everything."

"There is," said Rashaverak. "I know what you saw: I was watching."

"You mean? . . ." he gasped. His voice trailed away and he had to begin again. "Then what in God's name are my children?"

"That," said Rashaverak solemnly, "is what we are trying to discover."

—Arthur C. Clarke, *Childhood's End*

"I was having psychic experiences when I was a baby, before I could read. I can remember having experiences then of a dual consciousness. I was observing a very large ship sinking; lifeboats were coming away from it. I had a strong sense of having to try to do something. I was aware of the fear and the panic. It was nighttime, and the lights of the ship were going out, boats were pulling away, and the ship went down. I had this very strong impulse to seek help and remember clearly opening my eyes and seeing a crib, being completely disoriented, not knowing who or where I was, what I was doing in the crib or how old I was. I still thought that I was an adult, and I tried to speak. I wanted to tell the people in the room who must have been my parents that the ship had sunk, but the only thing that came out was a squeal and squeak, and within a few moments the adult sense was gone, and I remember nothing after that. I was very small.

"These experiences continued throughout my childhood. I remember when I was seven looking out the back window of the car, and the next moment the car and my body and everything around was inside me and I was looking down on it, but not as if I was looking from a height. It was my being that was aware of something inside me. That state then changed into another which had no visual impression to it—it was a sense of total identification with everything in the Universe. David Spangler ceased to exist: an entirely different consciousness took over. In that moment I knew who I was. I had a sense of the eternality of my existence, the fact that I was everything else as well. There was no limit to my identity; both the stars and the grass were me. It was one of those very cosmic experiences, it may not have lasted for very long, but it had a tremendous impact. I didn't talk about it, but it completely altered my frame of reference. It was an experience of waking up. I couldn't translate it into my seven-year-old consciousness easily. And from that point on, I have had a sense of being in two different dimensions simultaneously, of being in this one . . . and in another one."

David sipped slowly on a tall "Protein Drink" that ex-

Mormon Myrtle Glines, his spiritual partner, had brought in as a part of the morning ritual. The sun was shining brightly through the windows, and the heat, combined with the lulling timbre of David's voice, was making me drowsy. Within minutes, I was suffused with an almost mind-numbing tranquility and sleepiness as if I hadn't slept a wink the night before. And even realizing that the somniferous effect of David's voice is near-legend, I was still frustrated by it. Everything he was saying was fascinating, but I was stifling one yawn after another. It seemed almost an affirmation of David's "two dimensions" that he could speak so provocatively and yet, in ways mysterious, be a most effective soporific.

David has been called a lot of things: the Christ, the Avatar, a prophet. How does David respond to these tags? With humor. Humor is the most effective way he has found to deal with names and labels, and, more so, it is a way he often deals with the reality that he finds himself in. David seems to stand in one reality and humorously and gently unveil another with the easy wit that comes from absolute familiarity. He is so familiar with the invisible worlds of presences, beings, voices, guidance, that unlike mediums who become indignant when their credibility is called to question, David is one step ahead, making fun and laughing at himself.

When David walked through the gates of Findhorn in early summer 1970 there were about two dozen permanent members in the community. Pineridge did not exist except for Gillian Lubach's bungalow, next to Wilkie's Woods. Captain Ross Stewart had bought his bungalow, Joannie Hartnell-Beavis had one as well and was already assuming the responsibilities of treasurer, Elsie Dean was there, along with the Scales and Violet Barker, but there were hardly any young people.

Before coming to Findhorn, David and Myrtle had spent years together in various groups in California, she counseling and he giving hundreds of lectures. In the late sixties they gathered around them a group of people who shared the dream of "community," of an educational center that would be based on much of David and Myrtle's teachings. David had noticed how people who were willing to pay two dollars to hear a talk on spiritual life had an apparent unwillingness to actually apply the principles. Expressed in Spanglerese: "The higher destiny and potentialities of man were something to dream about and to look forward to, not something actively part of the here and now, demanding our creative attention and assistance for externalization and manifestation."

Before arriving, David did not know that much about Findhorn, although in the previous year Anthony Brooke had given him a copy of "The Findhorn Garden" and he recognized at once its potential as a living demonstration that spiritual principles are not airy abstractions but powerful and creative realities. David had seen New Age communes and communities forming and failing across the United States. They seemed to have "old age" qualities: egoism, competition, visionary impoverishment, lack of discipline and faith. Findhorn was different.

When he arrived at Findhorn in June of 1970, the caravan park was filling up with holiday visitors, and their brightly colored tents gave the old caravan park a medieval appearance. David had written ahead to Peter, little realizing that David's booklet about the Christ Experience in the New Age had preceded him by some three years and that Peter and Eileen had been waiting all this time for his arrival. The visit was intended to be a brief five-day one, but within hours David and Myrtle were aware of powerful vibrations of creativity and new direction that were grounded in the community. For both, it was a living example of the precepts they held for a viable spiritual community, a place where God was a living presence, a guiding reality joining with man in a creative partnership to bring Heaven down to Earth. The five days were extended to three years.

Within six months after David arrived, the community doubled in size to forty-five people, with young people pouring in until they outnumbered all the others. The Lightstone sisters came in through the sound barrier, singing at the top of their lungs. Jewels Manchester became Peter's "assistant," and her sister Merrily with husband Jim Bronson, fresh from Outward Bound school, started the photography and outdoor activities departments. Freya Conga joined Merrily in taking over the kitchen from Eileen and Joannie; a flock of artists moved in, starting a weaving studio, a pottery, a candlemaking workshop, and a graphic arts department. Alexis Maxcy began the drama group, while David, along with a Yugoslav artist, Milenko Matanovic, and American singer Lark Batteau started a vocal group called the New Troubadors. David began lecturing to the community several times a week in the "Park," a stone house adjacent to the caravan park. From these lectures sprang the "College" which David and Myrtle organized. From David's lectures came tapes and publications. The Troubadors wrote forty songs and recorded them for distribution. Jim Bronson and group turned out complete audiovisual presentations on Findhorn, the Elemental World, and several other related subjects. Victor Bailey with his father Arthur set the printing presses flying, and many new books came out: one more containing Eileen's guidance; a new one of Dorothy's; *The Findhorn News*; *Revelation, the Birth of a New Age* by David; and an expanded edition of "The Findhorn Garden." Pots, shawls, ponchos, candles, and prints were streaming forth from the studios and were being sold all over Scotland.

Findhorn expanded relentlessly, and growth was unchecked. The community had tripled in size by the end of 1972 to more than 120. And not surprisingly, personality conflicts and organizational challenges developed. Myrtle quietly stepped in, and through endless sessions of quiet counseling and sensible advice, she was able to help the younger members whose enthusiasm was creating the imbalance that almost tipped the ship. The majority of the personality clashes were between the younger people and Peter, and Myrtle, being the same age as Peter, was able to bridge the gap between the two and bring to individuals one by one a greater clarity in understanding the interaction of personality in a social organism. As a buffer between Peter and the creative members of the community, she became the mucilage that held the group together.

During this time, Findhorn almost went bankrupt, and from the holes in Findhorn's structure emerged a new structure, chartered around and centered in the consciousness of the group. Departments became "groups," and heads of groups became "focalizers," people whose purpose was to act as a lens within the whole in order to focus the energies generated by the group. Unity was sought through group "attunement"—a scoop of Maoism mixed well with an almost Quaker ethic, baked in the oven of Findhorn until well done. The creative burst that flashed through Findhorn almost tore it apart, but when the dust settled, it found itself to be a roaring community with twelve gardeners instead of two, with 170 people instead of fourteen, a large international mailing list—and inevitably, it found itself on the clipboard of the media. BBC filmed it four times, climaxing in the spring of 1973 with a one-hour prime-time color special televised live from the community center at Findhorn.

And after these came floods of letters and inquiries with visitors showing up from anywhere in the world at any time of the day. Accommodations were bursting, with seven people sometimes sharing one caravan; tents sprouted among the gorse bushes. Findhorn was on the map! Peter Tompkins came to gather information for his book *The Secret Life of Plants*, and when extracts from it appeared in *Harper's Magazine*, word began to circulate. William Irwin Thompson made Findhorn the last stop on his planetary pilgrimage, was transformed by David's lecture on the "Politics of Mysticism," and returned home to found a sister center in America called Lindisfarne. Like Tompkins, he devoted the last chapter of his book, *Passages About Earth*, to Findhorn and in particular to David Spangler, the enigmatic, twenty-eight-year-old sandy-haired youth who pranced about the community like a child and gave lectures which changed lives.

It is not easy to put your finger on what David has that gives him the ability to be an agent of individual and group transformation. If you ask him he will say that it is not he at all but a higher force. Whatever it is, the keynote is wholeness. Whenever David speaks, it seems as if he is always seeing a picture larger than you envisioned. And this wholeness of expression is evident in his balanced manner of speaking, of choosing words, and relating a story. When spiritualists talk about higher forces, beings, "upstairs," and other trade jargon to refer to a soul-infused state of being in touch with more exalted states of consciousness, an air of unreality and melodrama seems to belie their statements. When David speaks of the invisible world, of his contacts with a being called "John," or "Limitless Love and Truth," or Pan, he is so comfortable with that reality that you feel as if he is talking about a friend. He puts people at ease about topics that many find hard to accept.

David's qualities were recognized quite early in his life, and it was not long before a group called him the Christ, hoping to use his energies and ability to express spiritual truths to further its own aims. That opportunity, like all others which have promised David any measure of power, fame, or financial assistance, was turned down. This has left David without any tags, labels, or affiliations. The only thing you can call him is David Spangler. But, then, who is David Spangler? You are not going to worship him. If he is not channeling a cosmic being, he is reading comic books about them, or eating chocolate cake, or meditating under an electric blanket, or just being zany. His favorite pastimes include childish ones. The dual consciousness that began in the crib never fused, for he is still the child in some ways. But the being within him, or rather the being he is within, is profoundly disturbing and moving and has grown tremendously in stature from the passenger on the etheric ship twenty-seven years ago. He is mature and wise, and yet in the middle of a lecture he might crack an awful pun while retaining absolute composure. His creative output is staggering: lectures, writings, songs, singing, drama, plays; his wit is never-ending and constant; his positivity and love, abundant. In terms of personal revelation and the New Age, David embodies all that he speaks of.

David eventually left Findhorn, feeling that a continued presence there might lead to "devotional patterns" which would not be in anybody's best interest. In the spring of 1973 he returned to California to form with Myrtle and ex-Findhornians, the Lorian Association to carry out educational work oriented to the New Age. There he has remained except for occasional return visits. When I interviewed him he spoke of Findhorn with love but with some detachment as well, as if he wanted to make clear that Findhorn was Findhorn, and David Spangler was David Spangler, and the two identities should not be confused. He does not identify himself solely with Findhorn but rather with a larger network of emerging centers around the world, particularly in America.

David sees the significance of Findhorn as a demonstration that people can take the fate of the world into their hands, people whose vision of human destiny is vast, people who do not see man as a rudely treated element lost in a universe, but as a divine being who can draw from higher consciousness and attune to the will of God. In other words, Findhorn is a place where people become the plan rather than receive it in the Mosaic tradition from the mountaintops of religious bureaucracy. And this consciousness David would call planetary consciousness, differentiating it from an international consciousness, a consciousness of divisions, boundaries, separation, cultures, and geographies. Planetary consciousness transcends the cultural, national, and racial frameworks to merge with an awareness of the greater planet. It has no restriction in place or time but is derived from each individual touching upon the very essential part of our humanity which sees itself as integral with the greater whole of the planet. This is the consciousness emerging at Findhorn and at similar centers around the world, and Findhorn's role is to show that it can work, that it is not just another cute idea. Findhorn for David is not a community of people working and living together, but a "working organism seeking to accomplish what no human group has yet accomplished in the history of Mankind."

And what Findhorn seeks to accomplish, what in essence it has always sought to accomplish, and what it is accomplishing now is to sound the note, the first note of what will be a "mass planetary initiation." It recognizes that civilization as we know it is running solely on the energies of its own momentum and inertia. In a true Western sense, present-day society is lineal and therefore entropic, and David feels it is the first community to "solidly ground the energies of an entirely new *type*, not from new sources, but of a new vibration." No claim is made that Findhorn is the sole receptor of these energies. On the contrary, for the entire planet is seen as being bathed, suffused, and washed over by the light of a New Age. Each important cultural phenomenon today is in some way a recognition of this fact. New groups using new energies are reflecting entirely new patterns of thought. Old thought forms and cultural prejudices are being swept away with a speed and alacrity which may leave the world with a very bad case of nerves. Although these patterns can be destructive and even violent, they reflect a basic principle, which is that the old must pass before the new can arise.

The inability to fully recognize and comprehend the source and meaning of these "new energies" creates chaos and confusion. We see social phenomena as basic cause-and-effect occurrences reflecting cultural trends deeply seated in history and even racial memory. Without denying the validity of those relationships, David and many hundreds of thousands of others see and feel that the whole vibrational field which surrounds and suffuses the planet is in the process of undergoing radical changes. These changes, which uproot cherished ideals and old patterns of thought, can create a profound sense of discomfort and conflict in those who resist. But they can also give an overwhelming sense of harmony and peace to those who accept the new energies. The very polarization and divergence of the world, of its conflicts and schisms, whether they be religious, political, economic, sociological, or personal, are seen as the manifestations of one cause. New energies. Energies like the earth has never experienced before.

In one sense the New Age means an "age," because we are moving from one period of time to another, from the Piscean to the Aquarian. We know that the Earth moves through a 26,000-year equinoctial precession, and this precession, from our perspective, causes the equinoctial points to move backwards through the constellations, creating ages of approximately 2,100 years in length. An age is then the equinoctial month, and since it was 2,100 years ago that the equinoctial node moved from Aries to Pisces, we are coming to another transitional point. There are those who would say planets and constellations effect the differences in earthly energies, while others would say that they are only the visible measure of far vaster changes emanating from the infinite reaches of space. We live in a universal stream, and even the fiercest determinist would admit the possibility of the Earth's being affected by forces from space. What happens when we slightly change our orientation? The earth as a magnet slightly shifts; the cork bobs in the stream and slowly rolls on its side. What is the result? From celestial laws of mechanics we can plot the physical shifting of the planet, the "wobble," but there is no science that deals with the spiritual effect.

Prophecies of old have hinted, spoken, and sometimes shouted about what was going to happen in the latter part of this century. Books flood the market revealing the wisdom and knowledge of ancient cultures, the prophecies of "primitive" tribes, the wisdoms of native Americans. While there is some disagreement as to whether or not the changes the planet is undergoing will be accompanied by cataclysm and destruction, there seems to be less and less disagreement as to the reality of the changes.

Few can withstand the temptation at this apocalyptic point in man's evolution to turn pessimistic and gloomy. One of the most unusual aspects of David's philosophy is that it does not perceive any past patterns as being in error, as mistakes or as regressions. Nor does he perceive a "messiah" arising to save the world. In a sense what he is projecting and what Findhorn is projecting is a "myth." It is a new myth for man, projected into the collective consciousness, that will ultimately be transformed into reality. Both modern physics and Don Juan demonstrate the ineffableness of "reality." The thought that grows into the form is becoming the new reality as the causal laws of old science are increasingly less operative in our lives. The myth of Findhorn is the Myth of Creation, of a rebirth of man emerging into a totally new consciousness. The myth is not a few individuals gaining a higher understanding of the spiritual and cosmic principles behind life and creation, but a period when the planet as one shall begin to strip away the old personality patterns, the old thought forms, prejudices, and neuroses that distort the collective psyche, and in its place reveal the true divine nature of the planet. As with the individual, this new understanding and realization releases a great wave of energy and vitality into the planetary body, energy which further sweeps away the old and brings to the surface all that has to be cleansed and purified.

The Earth reborn is the myth and balances the Myth of Destruction which has invaded our consciousness and threatens to spill over into every waking moment. Destruction seen in the statistician's asymptotic charts of world collapse has resulted in mass escapism. Old world views are being replaced because they do not provide a working model for a new planet. They cannot explain the changes that are occurring every day. The institutions of the old culture are dead branches and cast-off leaves, while the tree remains, stripped to its trunk, seemingly dormant while renewing itself from the depths below. The old rots and becomes humus, soil for new growth.

The withdrawal of energies from the old world, the old cultural institutions, the old social configurations, is accompanied by a fortress mentality in those who would remain behind, those who protect and defend all that is "sacred." The ensuing conflict is like a man fighting his shadow. The inevitability of world collapse is heightened by this poignant drama of self-defeat. The powerful armies, the rather bizarre entities known as "multinationals," the rigid and doctrinaire governments suggest a planetary body lacking divinity which submits to a cancerlike disease, a body which destroys itself. We are armed to the teeth on a conscious level, ready to resist the rapid changes that carry in the New Age. We are like the man and woman who, justly or unjustly, choose to fight eviction every way they can rather than leave their derelict home. We will fight to the last before we release our ideas, the broken-down houses of old world memories.

What singles David out as a prophet is not his ability to perceive the patterns of dramatic world change—that he can do, but then so can many—but it is his pattern of conscious development that is quite different. He receives his information from higher realms, from beings who are extremely potent forces. And the presence who speaks to David most clearly and powerfully about Revelation and the New Age is one called Limitless Love and Truth.

"Am I God? Am I a Christ? Am I a Being come to you from the dwelling places of the Infinite? I am all these things, yet more. I am Revelation. [I AM] that Presence which has been before the foundations of the earth. . . . The earth . . . is My Body. I Am the Life from which all form springs. I Am the Womb and all must enter through Me. I Am not a Being. I contain all Beings. I Am now the Life of a new heaven and a new earth.

"I move steadily towards the consummation of My Revelation. For I attract to Me now lovers from beyond the stars to unite with Me and pour Their seed into Earth and transform it. I invoke and invite from beyond beings who come to impregnate Me with powers and energies from what I am beyond this system. [These beings and I] form the Body of a new heaven and . . . a new earth. [I draw] to Me the elements that will form the new heaven and the new earth and this motion proceeds . . . towards its perfect revelation. Your world shall become . . . two worlds. I Am the body of one; I Am the shepherd of the other. There are two worlds; one of the old, one of the new. Heed not the voices that speak to the old but know that I Am within you, for I would proclaim to you what comes from beyond. I would have you unite with it and be impregnated with it as I Am within you and receive from My greater Being beyond this planet."

According to David, two worlds is already a reality. The body of the old is fed by disintegrative energies, and those who tap into this are now experiencing at every turn the force of decay, collapse, and degeneration. Those who embody the new energies, receiving the seed from the "lovers beyond the stars," can and are creating a new world, grounding these energies into forms that will last and survive the coming period of world crisis. As this new world begins to emerge on the planet, the contrast between the two becomes more distinct, and individuals can more clearly perceive their conscious or unconscious alignment.

Although David has established a thesis of old and new, of two worlds separating, he goes beyond the form and reveals that the essence of the new age is within the consciousness of each individual. Findhorn is seen in this context as a garden for the growth of this consciousness, a place where old thought patterns are disintegrated in the deepest subconscious levels, where they become the "compost" of the ages, the potting soil which will nurture a new awareness and inner wholeness.

Findhorn's value is to demonstrate in practice the reality of New Age consciousness. It is not so much the forms that are remarkable as it is the consciousness that created those forms. And as a living demonstration, Findhorn sees itself as a "mother center" in that the lessons learned and demonstrated there can be applied in other centers. In other words, Findhorn is using these new energies right now, every day, in practical and pragmatic ways, demonstrating that the new is now, that the old is where your mind is. To those who wait for a sign of the start of the New Age, a cataclysm, the Edgar Cayce land shifts, a steaming Atlantis rising from the oceanic depths, David would say that the New Age is a seed point within every consciousness and the exploration begins whenever you wish. By concentrating on form, Findhorn is paradoxically demonstrating that the New Age is not form, that form is useful in that it is a reflection of consciousness. The temptation to look without and see the New Age in terms of a place is illusory. In a sense, Findhorn is one of the most outstanding examples of a New Age community, but by seeing it in that light only, we succumb to the very thought pattern of old which places form above consciousness, which separates matter from spirit, and the body from the soul.

There is a tendency among some to seek in Findhorn stability, and certainly some of the happiness that people initially feel when they arrive at Findhorn is a partial restoration of lost security. But according to David, Findhorn has something quite different to give. It gives impetus to the personality to release whatever it may be clinging to. In other words, real security is found when the personality level is reoriented to the soul, given up in a sense, and the only real constant that emerges from the flux is change itself.

That is not to say that there is no organizational structure within Findhorn, for in some ways there is more organization here than one might be accustomed to elsewhere. But it is based on organic models which take into account the principles of change and growth, both of the individual and of the larger whole of the group. Whereas the organizational patterns of the past were largely based on hierarchical authoritarianism and pyramidal patterns of control and leadership. Findhorn in keeping with the recognition of the divinity within all, is taking a different pattern, a pattern which David has called "synergy."

Synergy here means a social state in which the whole is greater than the sum of its parts. In other words, it is describing a state in which the individual in a group is greater than himself alone, with broader awareness and creative potential. Synergy is the opposite of the sacrificial modes of old which asked the individual to sublimate himself to the "highest good." The politics of synergy does not see the highest good beyond the individual but sees him embodying that highest good and bringing that embodiment into the greater whole, thereby enhancing it and the individuals belonging to it.

Synergy is a state of being, a social state, an energy state, in which the various units that form the component lives or elements all interact in such a way that no one unit wins out over the others and no one unit loses out to the others, but everyone gains; and as a result the whole is stronger, more efficient, better organized, and more life-fulfilling than it would otherwise be.

Social synergy requires a level of awareness which the personality does not have. It is an attunement to an energy which comprises the greater whole, an understanding that when two gather, they are more than two individuals, and ultimately they represent the potential of not only creating a greater oneness by pooling their individual talents and abilities but the potential of bringing heaven to earth, of accomplishing what "no human group has accomplished in the history of mankind."

To do this requires a constant reexamination of oneself and of one's awareness and attunement. The health of the organism does not depend on destructive criticism, but rather it depends on deep inner reflection and demonstration of those higher laws which man has been given down the ages. In this sense, Findhorn is not new at all. It may be called "Christian" if you like. But if it is Christian, then it is the Christianity Chesterton spoke of: "There is nothing wrong with Christianity, it is just that it hasn't been tried yet." And Findhorn is trying. Its role in planetary transformation will be in drawing out from its members the divinity within, not by technique or form, but by each individual being "My Name." The Magic is within us all, all the time. There is nothing at Findhorn that everyone does not have within himself or herself. The joy Find-hornians feel is not the joy of "we can do it better," but the joy of knowing that what they are doing is absolutely universal, that it can be done by any group, anywhere in the world today.

How to do it? David answers: "Re-cognize. Know again. There must be this openness of consciousness if we are to fulfill the reality of a 'New Age.' . . .

"Man's consciousness through the ages, from the moment when he first awakened as an individual and began to compare himself with his environment, has sought to become identified with the Divine processes flowing within himself so that he could be free, free to be the process and not an effect of the process, not a product of the process. That is what the 'New Age' is all about; man learning in consciousness to be the living process of the Divine in the moment, of himself in the moment, of what he is in the moment, and allowing everything else to take its place accordingly. As he becomes aware of what he is and what others are, as these are blended together, the forms become obvious. It makes little difference whether he is building a theater, a pot, or a cesspit; whatever he is building, it is the consciousness, the quality of the consciousness, that is important. Form is not so important except simply as an exercise in which consciousness can develop itself and learn to express itself.

"So the New Age is not any more important than any other age of man. It should not be looked upon as being the ultimate answer to all of man's problems, because the age itself is none of those things. Man is the ultimate answer to all of his problems; he always has been and always will be. It is what man does in and through his own being, his consciousness, and his openness to life. Therefore, out with the New Age, out with the old age, out with all ages, and in with agelessness, both personally, collectively, and in terms of our consciousness, for then we find the real spirit and essence of what the New Age is intended to convey. It is a time when man comes home again to his spirit and from that point accepts his crown and throne as the steward of life and the king of life, the king of his own life, and takes his place as a creative partner with God. He can then enter a new cycle, the momentum will grow, and change will indeed come swiftly, change upon change upon change until the only thing that is stable is the stability that we have created within ourselves. . . . Then we will discover that everything is stable and that there is no such thing as change, only that unfoldment of what is within us and the reorganization of matter to clear the way for that unfoldment and to allow it to express itself perfectly."

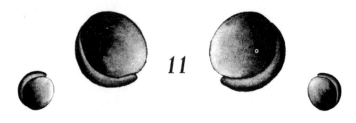

And the Light Catches You

As the Education Conference and my stay came to a close, the community broke into six groups of twenty people each in what was dubbed an Internal Conference. The focalizer of our group was Craig Gibsone, a rugged and handsome Australian who had spent two years at Findhorn. If you could think of Craig as a spiritual person, it would have to be something like a Robin Hood of the higher planes, for his function at Findhorn as Peter's assistant seemed to be the redistributor of energy. In every group he was part of, Craig seemed to draw out of each person and the group a vitality and spark. To the quiet and shy, he would pour out love and energy until they found themselves unexpectedly voluble. From the obtrusively demanding and controlling, he would draw out what they were really trying to say through their domination and need to direct. In short, he was a master of group dynamics.

Discussion proceeded easily in a wandering manner. The subjects covered were diverse, but each returned to one central theme, the sense of loss of self in terms of the personality, the new sense of sublimation to the greater whole and of being "attuned" to people who in fact one hardly knew at all. Although it would appear that within this context, talk is cheap, there existed within our group a greater measure of "oneness" than lip service. The Magic of Findhorn is the actual, palpable experience of one's own consciousness merging with a group consciousness. Discussions are not philosophical debates or expositions, but are more likely to consist of one individual after another describing the experience of oneness, the joy that this unfolding of consciousness bestows, and the lightness of mental gait when the load of being "someone" is cast away and the dance of simply being "one" begins.

The feeling in the room was very strong. A young Irish girl, who had met with us the day before and said nothing, now spoke. Her words were simple, but her whole body was shaking and every word was a great release of something held within for a long time. She said that she could not speak at first because she was so stunned to meet people like this; that she didn't believe people could "open up to each other" and share their very essence so easily and lovingly, and now she wanted to tell everyone how grateful and thankful she was. Still wanting to say more but unable to do so, she bowed her head and cried.

Someone here compared this process to "witnessing," where people recount their experiences of "Christ consciousness," of giving oneself over to Christ. Here Jesus is seen as a human embodiment of the Christ energy, not somebody nailed to the cross. In other words, he is a joyous messenger of God, a person who embodies and signifies transformation. Pain and suffering are absent from the Findhorn theology.

Although the community is conducive to transformation of consciousness, there are no techniques, meditations, dogmas, or physical exercises to bring this about, nor are there any gurus or benign and fatherly holy figures shedding their light and polishing tarnished souls. All the people I spoke to said that they have felt a greater sense of freedom here than they have ever felt before.

There is, however, a veritable host of invisible teachers,

and this ease and familiarity with the invisible world is unnerving. Not all people here are conversant with the world of spirit, but those who are tend to be very comfortable and relaxed about it, an attitude more common in Buddhist countries. Spiritual teachers at Findhorn are really "spiritual"; they are all spirit: Devas, Pan, Father Andrew, David's contact "John," the Archangel Michael, Saint-Germain, and so on. There is an extensive list, a resource the community draws upon through various people. I also began to hear references to space brothers, beings overlighting the planet. At this point my cultural cross reference to Oriental ancestor worship fell to pieces, and I felt that Findhorn was going to be impossible to "put to bed" journalistically. I was still trying to figure out the garden and how the community ran, and now it was space brothers.

But this direction of consciousness characterizes Findhorn's approach to everything: both eyes on heaven, both feet on the ground. "Bring heaven down on earth." That phrase pops up everywhere in the community, yet in practice it turns out to be difficult, and many people experience upheaval and turmoil in the attempt. The vibrant and powerful energy field that exists within Findhorn changes any individual who comes into it. When this energy flows into people, they find things coming out besides this energy. It is like sticking a powerful hose down a drain pipe. If the passage wasn't clean before, it soon will be. People here experience sudden and startling changes in their entire makeup and character, changes occurring so swiftly that they can be unsettling and disturbing at first. I have witnessed religious "conversion" before, but here there is no pressure to be anything except what you feel comfortable in being, and the effect is riotous. It's what Peter calls the greenhouse effect. People settle down into the greenhouse, operating in very ordinary ways, making pottery, weeding the lettuce patch, cooking lunches when they notice internal beanstalks they did not expect, have no way of controlling, and for which they have no reference. It is this rapid inner growth and change which throws people for ecstatic loops of tears or laughter.

Eileen has seen this time and again and has received guidance describing the process. "Be at peace. It is the opening of the heart center which makes you feel everything so deeply. You find that tears flow easily? These are the tears of joy—let them flow. They are the tears of recognition of Truth and Love Divine. This brings a feeling of elation, of thanksgiving, of a new and deep understanding. It is as if you had slept and have now awakened to find a new world. Everything looks different and beautiful, as if you went to sleep in winter when everything lay dormant and awakened to spring in its full glory."

The question that began to brew in my mind was not what Findhorn was doing to people—I could see that clearly enough all around me—but what was the Magic, what was the transforming power, what was the cause of this spiritual greenhouse, why did there seem to be such thick and vibrant energies whirling around the caravans and gardens? Everyone I talked to recounted a story of enormous personal growth within the community. No one had come here without being changed by the place, some from the moment they walked through the gates. The absence of a strong spiritual leader may indeed make the environment more conducive to change and growth, but it did not explain what was the agent of this change. Peter flatly denied it was himself, and Eileen appeared to be a contemplative and dutiful wife, whose time was divided between meditation and hostess duties; ask her about religion or matters esoteric, and she will wave her hand and say, "I don't know a thing about all of that stuff."

Whatever it is, it is everywhere. It seems to be in the very physical stuff of the place. If you walk across the road to the bay, it is not quite there. Standing by the bay is beautiful, but the intense energy field of Findhorn is missing. Everybody here talked about it, knew about it, referred to it as "the energies," and yet when I asked individuals what this transforming power was, everyone gave different answers. Some said it was "love," some said it was "Christ energies," others said it was caused by the changes in the "etheric web" of the planet.

Those statements gave me little satisfaction, particularly since I was beginning to feel it myself. All attempts at reportage and detached observation were being washed down my drain pipe, and in their place was growing a feeling of "being home." It was the first place in my life where I felt comfortable with such a diverse collection of people. For someone who had been a "lone wolf" all his life, slipping in and out of situations by the back door, looking and watching, observing and waiting, I found myself being drawn into the thick and heady atmosphere of what could only be called pure and unadulterated joy.

When I left the States for Findhorn, the community (overlooked for so long because it wasn't near India) was already in the underground rumor mill. Friends wrote wanting to know if anything was "going on up there"— something is most definitely going on, but the problem was that I could not find anyone in the community who could adequately explain it to me. If you have ever visited a room where a saint or holy man has lived and meditated, you know that feeling of experiencing a presence which defies analysis. At Findhorn that presence is strong and powerful, and anyone can notice it. It seems to be a place where divine energy is anchored, an energy which flows through everything, from the flowers and the children to the elderly people in their eighties. People who cannot accept it leave. The problem is not in getting people to leave, but what to do with those who want to stay, for there is simply not enough room.

On the afternoon after the conference, as I was packing

for my departure the next day, Peter came in with great stacks of material. "Take this and read it through—it may be of some help to you. These are unpublished things, transmissions from Saint-Germain, Sir Francis Bacon, and a private report on Iona by David Spangler. It will help you see the significance Findhorn has to Britain and the planet." And with that air of suppressed excitement that he carries about him always, Peter gave me a large grin and took off.

I sorted through the material. Much of it had come "through" David as transmissions, and there was a rather stern and no-nonsense message from one Master Rakoczi:

You are each here to demonstrate the reality of the spiritual nature of man and of its possibilities and potentials released through an attuned consciousness and through action guided by intuition and love and wisdom. There is a strong force of will, of purpose, moving through this centre which will accomplish all the objectives for which the centre was founded. It is not dependent on any individual. Individuals may attune to it and find their own life enhanced, make their own contribution to the whole and in turn find their wholeness increased. Or individuals may be unable to attune to it, in which case they will be unable to stay.

The stakes are high and time grows increasingly short, and as the time grows shorter the freedom that we have to work and to alter events in human consciousness becomes less and the probabilities of certain actions taking place becomes greater. For every moment of the Earth's turning in which forces of emotional imbalance, instability, negation and hatred flourish or manifest themselves, your world is brought that much closer to a point of judgment and collapse. There is a time established in the last quarter of this century, a time which cannot be revealed, when you will be confronted as a planet with a major crisis with

smaller ones leading up to it. How well mankind moves
through that depends on what is done now to build the new
patterns, for it is within the structure of light that will be
established and is being established now, that you and we
will have the freedom to work and to influence human
events . . . the extent of the new society you can develop
in these months and years will determine how critical and
how destructive the years ahead of you will be, from a
human point of view.

Peter's faith in me was sterling. Did he not know that I
was frankly and unabashedly skeptical of such stuff? But I
found myself enjoying it anyway, in spite of my doubts.
The *Iona Report* caught my eye next.

It was written in outline style with parts and lettered
subheadings. The first part was entitled "Introduction:
Power Points, the Etheric Web and the Significance of
Iona." In the report, David Spangler expressed a theory
similar to John Michell's *View Over Atlantis*: a Britain
dotted with "power points" connected together by "ley
lines" all of which are the extensions of an "etheric web"
encircling the globe. The etheric web is analogous to the
vital energy of the human body which is called Ch'i in the
Orient and is manipulated in acupuncture. This etheric
energy is the matrix from which forms emerge into denser
planes of existence. The webbing has been described by
certain seers and clairvoyants who can see these energy
fields as thousands of interlinking golden strands. Just as
the body has certain centers, chakras, and pressure points
where this energy concentrates and accumulates, the earth
is dotted with power points where the etheric energy is
grounded into the earth. At these points, the etheric energy
can be used and transformed by human beings into vital
energies of growth and development. These centers cor-
respond to various manifestations of etheric energy with
differing functions.

These power points are the meeting place between two dimensions. In that interface where the veil is thinnest, man can most easily experience contact with other forms of consciousness. If the energies of a power point are properly anchored and stabilized, then they can be used to influence life on the planet, particularly in the surrounding area.

What David sees as happening now is a release of new energy from the etheric web into the earth, particularly into new centers formed for that very purpose, like Findhorn. When you convert a home from coal to electricity, you have to change the fittings and devices which are to receive this new energy; similarly, the consciousness of man must change in order to fully receive the New Age energies. This explains the apparent gap between those people who are attuning themselves to these energies and reflecting an attitude of love, peace, and harmony and those who cannot imagine what these people are talking about. It also explains how someone can one day be a straight officeworker and the next moment have experiences which completely alter his or her makeup. What happens? Is it possible that in idly tuning the dial of their consciousness they discovered a new channel?

The lives of the residents of Findhorn are littered with the husks of successful careers, jobs, and professions. The drop-out movement of sixties' youth is now transgenerational. Living within the community are the Reverend and Lieutenant Colonel Stephen Field, Flight Lieutenant Richard Barton and Captain Ross Stewart, R.N., Justice of the Peace, and John Hilton, a former bank manager. There are ministers, architects, plumbers, screenwriters, nurses, electricians, a physician, ex-junkies, a soccer star, and a biologist.

What happened? People are not coming to Findhorn to grow gloxinia, or for a dive into the esoterics that Peter represents. They have come to experience God, and like their brethren around the globe who have ferreted out ancient techniques of consciousness alteration, they are the new travelers seeking in their journeys that point of departure where they might leave their earthbound consciousness behind and fuse with a greater one, inclusive of the earth, the consciousness of God.

When you become a member you are being accepted by an organism, and it is the entire organism that is trying to experience a new consciousness. You become a part of something greater than yourself, and the experience of God at Findhorn is done within the context of the greater whole. This does not deny personal revelation, but enhances it. Within the greenhouse of Findhorn there is an atmosphere where processes of inner change and unfoldment are greatly speeded up. The love and attention given the garden is surpassed by the love and attention that each individual shares with others—Findhorn as a group is comparable to a spiritual petri dish culturing a new consciousness.

The comforting thing about Findhorn is that even it does not fully comprehend what is happening here. An air of spontaneity and openness pervades which is refreshing and invigorating. There is not an ancient Codex breathing thick and heavy rules and orders into the youth, nor does Findhorn have a game plan, some vast scheme which it is seeking to fulfill. The faith felt here is strong, and even in disbelief, you welcome it. Anxious mothers and fathers who have flown in from the States to investigate their daughters' latest folly have been transformed within hours and have left weeks later more dedicated than their off-spring. Dedicated to what? Love? Findhorn? Devas? All and none of these things, for what you take away from Findhorn is a new way of seeing—one cannot remain here for long and not be filled with a new hope for mankind.

There is a certain cogency when someone at Findhorn speaks of "the new," for the person invariably embodies on both internal and external levels the newness of which he speaks. One has had to remake himself in order to fully "attune" to these new channels. It is not that he is a follower of a way or path outlined by another individual, but rather, each person has listened to that voice within himself and followed it, some obediently, some kicking and fighting all the way. Within every person here is that knowing, that very special understanding of what led each person to the north of Scotland. That knowing is the seed from which the harmony of the group grows, overcoming barriers that separate people.

Findhorn is, according to David, a power center. While similar to the power points of old, it is not a part of the ancient etheric web. It is anchoring energies of an entirely new vibration, energies which do not come through a hierarchy of priests and kings. Everyone here is expected to be his own priest and king—there are no subjects, followers, or chelas. David sees another basic difference between Findhorn and the power centers of old: "The value of the New Age centers is that they are developing around people and places relatively uncontaminated by the thought forces, energies, and patterns of the past. Not being a part of the old web of power lines and influence, these new centers are not faced with having to overcome the inertia and ambiguous energies from past patterns. Thus a new world is being born and shall be born, and an old world, an ancient world of energy and forces, is dying and falling away."

It was four in the afternoon by the time I finished the *Iona Report*, and I decided to go for a run and a swim. I took off up the road through the community and Pineridge, around Wilkie's Woods and onto the gorse- and heather-covered shingle ridges leading to the beach. The sun was obscured by massive clouds that clogged the sky. For October, it was an unusually warm afternoon, and when I arrived at the beach, not seeing a soul in sight, I took off my clothes and jumped in.

After dressing, I walked back toward Wilkie's Woods.

Walking slowly over an embankment of sand and into the bottom of the depression, I experienced a great stillness, as if I had walked into a forest thicket. The grass was luminous, the moss like green embers scattered across the sandy floor. Light played on the sand, and each particle was a crystal refracting the sun in a sparkling white and gold diffusion of lines and beams. The lines of light held me entranced, caught by the unexpected beauty of a place which had formerly looked like a desolate wasteland.

The light focused in my mind's eye into one bright light. I saw other points of light forming around the earth. The first light I had seen then became the hub of a wheel around which the other lights now turned, and slowly the earth-wheel transformed into a translucent body within which the wheel still turned, and the lights became the chakras and points of energy on the body. The scene changed again, and every light diminished and seemed to fly away into the cosmos and space, taking its place among the constellations in the blackness, leaving a starlit sky in my vision which then became the crystal sand touched by a setting sun.

The points of light on the planet were like seeds, each one representing a different aspect of consciousness, and each one being a seed for a new life, a new birth, a new race of men. The experience took Findhorn beyond the world of sects, teachers, and groups, and in that moment I realized the natural quality of what was taking place.

It seemed that Findhorn was a mutation, that the whole of the community was an organism that had sprung to life on the planet against many odds. Like some primitive species that arose out of the primeval ocean billions of years ago, Findhorn represented an emergent aspect of the evolution of consciousness on the planet. Far away from the cities, the pollution, the strange vibrations and cultural forms of civilization, desolate in a way, Findhorn was located where the air, water, and land were pure and, as

David said, the ethers were pure as well. All the new words, the teachings, the people like Peter, David, and Eileen, seemed at once to be organic manifestations of the whole. I knew that they had not decided anything, that they had not created anything, but had co-created it, seeing with clarity the vision that existed there, and acting as one with the emergent organism to bring it to life and fruition.

The world of plants brought the world of spirit into a dimension that could be comprehended. I saw all of the strange jargon as inadequate verbal tools trying to express something greater. I could see how people would dismiss with a wave of the hand the occult and New Age teachings, but at Findhorn, and especially in that moment, the unreal became real, the extraordinary became ordinary. The penny finally dropped. There were still a thousand questions in my mind, but at least I had a nascent sense of what this transforming energy was. And having sensed it, I could understand why people could not describe it. Peter's words, "You cannot describe Findhorn, you must experience it," came to life. It occurred to me that it wasn't important whether it was described or not. After all, it was here, people were coming and going, sharing and growing, and Findhorn was expanding in a natural enough way.

I had wondered why within Findhorn there was the absolute absence of dogma and proselytization. I knew then that it was because there was nothing to preach, nothing to defend, nothing to hold on to. At Findhorn, people talk about planetary service, yet demonstrate it in their everyday life by emptying ashbins and selling potatoes in the shop. It is not what they do—it is the manner in which everything is done. It is the extraordinary care, love, and dedication that you see in Don taking care of a patron at the store, or in Richard when he pours a concrete slab, or in Joannie when she counts the sheets and towels, or in all the people here living their daily lives, serving the whole, knowing that God and they are one.

The following day was spent busily tying up loose ends and saying goodbye to new friends. In the afternoon, Craig asked if I would go for a short drive. We went toward Forres, turning off on a side road winding through a thick forest. Parking in the dirt under a large beech tree, Craig announced our destination: the "power point" of Cluny Hill. As we slowly walked up the tree-covered Druid Processional, I was full of apprehension as to what I was supposed to be experiencing. What happens at a power point? Past the dripping trees and blackberry bushes we silently climbed until we stood on a rather scruffy area on the side of the hill. I could see far inland to the Cairngorms, while down below came the faint cries of golfers on the Forres course. I closed my eyes, as it seemed the proper thing to do, and Craig and I stood silently. When I opened my eyes, Craig was looking at me, with the same dining room expression of my arrival night. I had experienced nothing, just the deep and silent peacefulness of the woods and hills. I closed my eyes again, and sank back into the stillness. A few minutes later, we were on our way back down the hill, Craig saying or asking nothing, me wondering if I hadn't missed something again.

When we got back to Findhorn, Peter was waiting, for we had just enough time to return to the Forres train station. We climbed into the car after I had fetched my bag and kissed and embraced a dozen people, and we sped off with only minutes to spare, Peter jauntily going 75 miles an hour through the misty rain. Craig and he were in the front seat laughing and carrying on like brothers, while I sat in the back still wondering if I had missed something that afternoon.

We arrived at the station minutes before the wooden-seated electric that would take me to Inverness arrived. It gave us precious few moments to say goodbye, but that was just as well, for I was feeling uncomfortable and wondered what to say. I really didn't want to leave Findhorn or new friends, and it made the farewells that much more awkward and uneasy. I was suddenly wishing I was a member, not relishing the thought of the journey back to an urban American winter. I was frantically thinking of how to express this to Peter when the whistle blew and I clambered aboard. Craig and Peter were still waiting, so I opened the window and poked my head out. Peter grinned and said, "We expect you back," and waved, taking slow steps away from the moving train. I followed them with my eyes until a bend in the tracks took them from sight.

I had got on the first-class car by mistake and found it empty. The engineer was two rows ahead of me on the other side of a glass partition, leaning over a poorly rolled cigarette and the *Daily Mail* football page, reminding me of my crofter seen in burning fields—the same sunken cheeks, bitter eyes, broken veins, and etched face under colorless hair. On the front page of the paper he was holding was one word: CRISIS.

I looked out the window to the tower on Cluny Hill with the thought of headlines mingling with the peace and stillness I had experienced. It occurred to me that the "power" of Cluny Hill was that very quiet that touched the depths of my being, and that the name had misled me into expectations of far-out happenings and revelations. The revelation and power was the peace that I found within myself, and in a world where crisis had become household, it seemed the most precious gift of all.

Notes and Comments

Many of my impressions of the Scottish countryside were a trackside view from a weary eye. I have returned to Scotland twice since then, and have experienced it as a country of rare and singular beauty. I would appeal to my ancestral countrymen indulgence for those first impressions.

Space, continuity and time prevented me from dealing with many aspects of the community, past and present. It is still a vast subject, one which I have only touched upon. One important and vital relationship in the development of Findhorn was the one between Peter and David, a relationship which I am told embodied the deepest expression of love and trust. It would seem that the coming together of these two widely different personages was the key to Findhorn's rapid growth and expansion in the seventies. Since David was no longer a member of the community when I arrived, it was a relationship that I was unable to observe or experience, but its effects and contribution to the whole are evident everywhere at Findhorn.

Sheena Govan was not the woman portrayed in Chapter Four and Eileen would be the first to agree. Readers should note that the descriptions of Miss Govan and of the Isle of Mull reflected the inner turmoil Eileen was experiencing at that time. Sheena did not see much of the Caddys after she returned Christopher. In the following year, she suffered the unfortunate distinction of being singled out by the more sensational tabloids in Scotland and England for her unorthodox spiritual views. This occurrence and the increased frequency of her headaches compelled her to seek a more reclusive existence as a music teacher. She died some years later of a brain hemorrhage. Poor and largely forgotten, she is still remembered with reverence by those of Findhorn whose lives she so profoundly touched.

In Chapter Three, Fosco Maraini's book *Secret Tibet* provided a rich description of the passage between Kalimpong and Gyantse from which I was able to corroborate impressions received from Peter. The italicized quotation on page 52 is by Milarepa and is taken from Mr. Maraini's book. The quotation in capital letters on page 54 is from the Book of Dyzan in *Isis Unveiled* by Madame Blavatsky; the quotation on page 58 is from the Evans-Wentz translation of the *Tibetan Book of the Dead*; italicized sections on pages 61–62 and 68 are from interviews with Peter Caddy. The italicized section of page 54 however is my own words.

All italicized sections and quotations from Chapter Four are reconstructed from extensive interviews with Eileen Caddy about her experiences on Mull, except the guidance which is taken directly from her book *God Spoke to Me*.

Italicized sections on pages 108, 110–111 and 114–115 in Chapter Six are quoted from the manuscript of a book Dorothy Maclean is writing about her experiences with the Devic Kingdom. All other italicized sections are Deva messages directly from her Deva transcripts.

The verse beginning Chapter Seven is from Tolkien's *The Tree and the Leaf*, and although no source is given by Tolkien, several Scotsmen agree that it is a ballad of old. The quoted material in Chapter Seven is taken directly from a piece written by Roc for the original *Findhorn Garden* pamphlet, except for parts of the text on pages

129, 130 and 131 which are amplifications of the original text as given in interviews by Roc.

Quotations in Chapter Nine by Sir George Trevelyan, Lady Mary Balfour, and Sir Lindsay Robb are also taken from the *Findhorn Garden* book. The quotations of Donald Wilson on pages 171–172 are from correspondence received by Peter Caddy. Lady Eve Balfour's comments were given in an interview at the University of Reading. Marcel Vogel's statement was given in an interview during his visit to the community in 1974.

Finally, the quotations of David Spangler on pages 179–180 were given in interviews at his home on San Carlos, California. The quotation on page 191 is from *Revelation: The Birth of a New Age*. The last quotation on pages 194–195 were taken from a lecture given by David during his visit to the community in the winter of 1973 entitled "Growth, Authority, and Power."

Anyone wishing to write to the Findhorn Community should address their correspondence to: Findhorn Foundation, The Park, Findhorn Bay, Forres, Moray, Scotland.

One final word about the community. Findhorn is a dynamic and living organism, and like everything today, it is changing and growing constantly. To try and capture the present "reality" of Findhorn is an endless task as it never ceases to amaze and surprise all those within and without with its changes. If you should ever have the opportunity to visit the community, do not go expecting that which you have read in this book or any other publication. Simply go with an open heart and the centeredness of your own being and you will undoubtedly have the most fulfilling of experiences.

Acknowledgments

This book would not be complete without the recognition of the many people whose contributions made it possible. It was the faith of my editors, Robert Hargrove and Buz Wyeth, that gave me the confidence to write the book. Aidan Meehan caught the vision at the outset and provided me with an endless stream of ideas from his vivid imagination. The initial stages of research were well attended by Elizabeth Hagensen and Roxanne Strobe who spent hundreds of hours transcribing interviews. Both were extremely patient and supportive, a gift gratefully received as we proceeded.

Findhorn members, past and present, demonstrated their support in countless and varied ways. A particular debt of gratitude is owed to Hans Poulsen for his universality and love, to Will and Pat Carlseen for smiles and coffee, to Don and Ann Zontine, Jon and Joy Drake, David Sutherland, Joannie Hartnell-Beavis, Gwen Coy, June Hurly, Kathy Thormod, Hamish MacKay, Scott Goldberg, Alice Weibull, Jim and Pat Quigley, Stephen and Suzanne Brown, Jill and Angus Marland, Pam and Andy Thomas, Mick and Joseph Colton, Richard Valeriano, Gair Hemphill, to Gillian Lubach for her balance, Mary Hilton, Elsie Dean, Jenny Walker, Elizabeth Beattie, Michael and

Simone Worth, Margie Elliot, Leonard Powell, Michael Lindfield, Sally Walton, Lyle and Elizabeth Schnadt, Anastasia Sutherland, John and Janet Willoner, Mary Coulman, Chris Connolly, John and Judy Deming, Tom Earle, Marshall and Hazel Spangler, Mr. and Mrs. Ross Stewart, Victor and Sarah Bailey, Roy and Muriel McVicar, Jonathan, David and Christopher Caddy, Robin Gormley, Jerry Houck, Alan Splet, Mary Inglis, Richard Stern, Craig Gibsone, Jewels Manchester, Lark Batteau, Milenko and Freya Matanovic, Jim and Linda Glines, Roger and Catherine Collis, Greg Smith, Karen Hogg, Evelyn Sandford, Crispin Currant, Raymond and Celeste Akhurst, David Elliot, Cheryl Barker, Jim and Rosemary Hill, Frank Stong, Nevena Silic, Howard, Cathy and Patti Lightstone, Frank Bahnson, and especially "Gerry."

A special mention to the Lorian Association members who shared their spirit and joy so beautifully in word and song. David Spangler and Myrtle Glines were very helpful and generous with their time, giving a rare glimpse into the past of Findhorn and a view that was whole and complete. Dorothy Maclean was a delight to be with and added a much needed perspective to the story and history. During my stay in California, Jim and Merrily Bronson proved to be the most gracious of all hosts, their kindness and love saying more than words could about their experiences at Findhorn.

Three members of the community, John Hilton, Lisa Stern, and particularly Shoshana Tembeck proofread initial drafts and provided valuable insights, positive criticisms, and a loving touch, which rescued the book from numerous clichés, overwrites, and other awkwardisms. All played a major role in the final form it took.

Peter and Eileen Caddy were remarkable in every respect, giving of their time at all times of the day, meeting my every need, assisting and helping with all aspects of the book, and in sharing their lives with a purity and honesty that was a teaching in itself. Their lives breathed and embodied all that Findhorn stood for. Their dedication and selflessness would serve as a fitting model for any venture in community and group living. I am not only indebted to them for the energy they poured into the book, but for the experience of having known two of the finest people I've ever met.

Roc was equally generous with his time and self, sitting for long interviews which contained such a wealth of fascinating information that a book could be written just about him. He was a man full of wisdom and insight, steeped in humility and grace.

The two-paragraph fancy about the Devas of the Fire, Earth and Wind in Chapter 6 were directly inspired by Mathew Shields whose insights into the garden were a continuous source of understanding.

Alexis Maxcy provided me with a wealth of insightful information about the community and key members. His humor and incisive views combined with his wit gave endless hours of delight and laughter, for which I am very grateful. Lady Mary Balfour, Lady Eve Balfour, Marcel Vogel, and Sir George Trevelyan gave of their time in interviews and discussions, providing unique and valuable perspectives.

Lorrayne Thompson and Nicky Vardy gave graciously of their time and energy, typing for many days the various drafts. Their comments and observations proved valuable and perceptive while their presence was a delight. Bill Tara and Jeremiah Lieberman played special roles in getting things started. Fred Rohé, my spiritual teacher and fellow writer, planted the seeds of authorship years ago, and has been an inspiration throughout my life. I am grateful to the staff of Erewhon and to Tom Chappell for providing support during the year it took to complete the book. A very special note of appreciation is owed to Lynne McNabb at Harper & Row who was so helpful and cooperative during the finishing stages of the book. If everyone were as joyful as she to work with, it wouldn't be called work anymore.

Of all the community members who actively participated and helped, it was Dobrinka Popov who became my most faithful and beloved assistant. It was not only the weeks she spent in typing and re-typing, and the hours of proof-reading that she selflessly gave, but towards the end, when the days were long and the book began to assume seemingly endless proportions, it was Binka's love and unfailing happiness that carried us through to the end.

A special word of thanks to Abbott and Danny Johnson and Victoria Mudd for giving space and quiet to edit and proof the finished manuscripts.

And finally, from its earliest point, it was a very beautiful person whose patience and understanding gave what was needed. Although our paths were to part during the writing of the book, Dora is still the foundation upon which it began. There is no way of expressing that knowing and that gratitude in words.

This book is to be returned on or before
the last date stamped below.

WITHDRAWN